Civil Society in Action

Civil Society in Action

Global case studies in a practice-based framework

John Beauclerk, Brian Pratt and Ruth Judge

INTRAC, the International NGO Training and Research Centre, was set up in 1991 to provide specially designed training, consultancy and research services to organisations involved in international development and relief. We aim to improve civil society performance by strengthening management and organisational effectiveness, and by exploring policy issues.

First published in 2011 in the UK by:
INTRAC
Oxbridge Court, Osney Mead
Oxford
OX2 0ES
United Kingdom
Tel: +44 (0)1865 201851
Email: info@intrac.org
Website: www.intrac.org

Copyright © INTRAC 2011

ISBN 978-1-905240-17-3

Designed and produced by Jerry Burman
Tel: 01803 845562

Printed in Great Britain by Antony Rowe, Chippenham, Wiltshire

Cover image © RASTA 2008

Contents

Acknowledgements		1
Foreword		3
Chapter 1	Introduction	7
Chapter 2	Building the social basis for democracy	21
Chapter 3	Promoting political accountability	37
Chapter 4	Producing trust, reciprocity and networks	53
Chapter 5	Creating and promoting alternatives	69
Chapter 6	Supporting the rights of citizens and the concept of citizenship	83
Chapter 7	How to support civil society over the next decade	97
Appendix 1	Beyond NGOs: Components of civil society – distinguishing between NGOs, CSOs and social movements	117
Appendix 2	Who rules: the citizen or the state? Theoretical debates over civil society	121
Appendix 3	Example of civil society mapping in Ethiopia	127
Chapter endnotes		131

Acknowledgements

The first and foremost thanks must go to the representatives of civil society who presented case studies of their work at the December 2008 INTRAC conference 'Whatever Happened to Civil Society?'. These cases provided the base material for this book, and we are very grateful to them for contributing to the conference, and graciously granting us permission to discuss their cases here.

Sincere thanks, in the order in which their case studies appear, to: Asiya Sasykbaeva of the Center Interbilim; Konstantin Kovtunets of INTRAC Central Asia; Dr Monica Banerjee of the National Foundation for India; Alvaro Caballero of CIRD; Beverley Jones; Caroliza Peteros of the Mediators Network for Sustainable Peace; Evans Wafula; Njundu Drammeh of the Child Protection Alliance; Dee Jupp; Rajesh Tandon of PRIA and Marcella Tam of PSO; Lucy Earle of the University of Cape Town; Adriana Sánchez González of the Cooperativa Sulá Batsú R.L.; Sharda Ganga of Stichting Projekta; Uche Igwe of EITI and Carol Ballantine of Trocaire; Arifur Rahman of the Manusher Jonno Foundation; Silvia Guimarães Yafai of the Building and Social Housing Foundation; Rachel Julian; Omana T Kochukuttan of RASTA; Karoline Kemp with ISS-Hivos; Ivan Garcia of the Coordinadora Civil de Nicaragua; Henry Armas with ISS-Hivos; Barry Cannon; and Doug Reeler of CDRA.

This book would not have been possible without the generous financial support of Sida, the Swedish International Development Cooperation Agency, which enabled both the initial conference and the subsequent work on this book; The Dutch Foreign Ministry and Cordaid, who supported the initial conference; and Kepa and Save The Children Sweden, who sponsored conference participants. Many thanks to Zoe Wilkinson, whose hard work on the logistics of the conference played a big part in making it such a success.

Many thanks also go to the thoughtful commentators whose insights helped to refine the book: Rod McLeod, Brenda Lipson, Rick James, Janice Giffen, Kaustuv Bandyopadhyay, Andy Clayton, and Pim Verhallen.

Foreword

At an INTRAC conference in 2008, we started the process of looking at the nature and role of civil society, under the title 'whatever happened to civil society?'. Many people have asked why. Neither this question, nor the question posed by the conference title, are easy to answer. The conference, and this book, are an attempt to review what is actually happening under the guise of 'civil society', and what this means.

John and Brian started working in development in the 1970s together in Peru, where we worked with social movements – indigenous peoples, peasant unions, community action groups – to help them develop with and for their members. We understood then that to resolve long-term structural poverty we had to engage with the processes of political economy rather than just provide services for ameliorating the symptoms of that poverty. Years later, the development sector has been converted into a massive business supplying a huge range of services, where the growth of NGOs had become the single most quoted indicator of success. In the past 30 years we have seen a proliferation in the use of the words 'civil society', the creation of official donor 'civil society departments', and most recently even a 'big' civil society initiative fostered by a northern state. However we feel that the rhetoric of growth has not been accompanied by the crispness of purpose we previously enjoyed, and there is actually less support for civil society itself as a broader force in society, as opposed to the use of organisations, primarily NGOs, to deliver on aid for the aid industry.

It is precisely because of this we feel it important to ask 'whatever happened to civil society?' Whilst in the past we often filled gaps in services in very poor communities, on the whole the model was one of supporting local community structures, priorities and initiatives. Since then, we often wondered what had happened to the principle of supporting local groups, of keeping our own input to the minimum. As the debates turned to scaling up direct services by NGOs, and NGOs became institutions not support organisations, we wondered whether civil society had, in part, become absorbed into the aid industry.

This book can be criticised for falling into the same trap that is the subject of our critique, as we use the experiences of northern and southern NGOs to illustrate our ideas. This is due to the fact that both the authors and many of our colleagues have 30-40 years' experience of working with NGOs; this is the world we have inhabited and contributed to.

We will make the argument that whilst international aid has done many positive things, it has led to an imbalanced growth of 'aided' civil society compared to 'unaided' civil society. It is important to remember that the resources flowing to and through civil society are a historically short phenomena. Whilst civil society in various forms has existed for centuries, the channelling of funds across international boundaries under the form of international cooperation towards civil society is a very recent development.

This success has brought with it problems, as many civil society groups have grown rapidly beyond their original visions and missions, and possibly their ability to manage themselves. Other groups have sprung up as a direct result of international cooperation, have never known a base outside this system, and hence don't see its ephemeral nature. This is not to say that there have not been great successes through funding social movements; one can point to the many examples of peasant unions, indigenous groups supported in Latin America in Brazil and the Andes. It is possible to support civil society without inevitably directing it into a homogenous aid model.

Some of the problems with the prevailing approach to civil society can be seen in countries which move away from being recipients of aid as they reach middle-income status. Whilst at one level this is something to celebrate, it also presents a whole new set of challenges. The foremost challenge which concerns us is: how does civil society make the transition from being aided to continuing its roles, unaided by foreign funds? Whilst there is more still to be reviewed and analysed in this area, this book starts from a hypothesis that despite the positive work over the last 30 years, the aid industry's idea of civil society has been hijacked by the professionally funded NGO. In doing so the idea of civil society has been tied into other debates about development and the aid industry, leading to some of its important elements being forgotten, obscured or lost. We hope to contribute to its rediscovery with the help of the case studies in the book.

We believe that the framework we have developed and the case studies presented will help us move away from regarding civil society as primarily about meeting the instrumental needs of the aid industry. It is unashamedly an attempt to go back to the origins of the concept and importance of civil society as a socio-political construct which engages our lives, whoever and wherever we are.

This approach is not designed to undermine the very good work that many organisations have achieved, as illustrated by the case studies we are able to share, which are only a small proportion of the great work done by NGOs and other civil society groups across the globe. Instead, what we hope is that these case studies help illustrate how this work can support a broader civil society in productive ways. These case studies also illustrate the importance of the wider functions of civil society and how some groups have managed to work within them.

More than 40 case studies were presented at the initial conference and these, plus the accumulated experiences of INTRAC and our partners, have contributed to the ideas in the book. We hope that the book makes an initial step towards the reconsideration of the nature and role of civil society – namely, that it is absolutely crucial as an end in itself. We also hope that it promotes thinking on how civil society's various roles may best be protected, promoted and strengthened, especially in contexts – including in the global north – where its independence is under threat from cooptation by the state and the private sector. As international aid leaves many countries, have we been able to strengthen and support civil society, or have we left it vulnerable once the financial lifeline is removed?

If we are able to contribute to once more putting civil society and its citizens back into the development debate as independent actors, then we will have achieved something. We need to look towards a very different way of working with civil society, especially those most marginalised by present political and economic systems.

The authors would like to thank everyone whose work contributed to this book, especially the original case study presenters named in the acknowledgements. We take final responsibility for any errors, and the views expressed in general.

John Beauclerk, Brian Pratt and Ruth Judge, December 2010

Introduction

Whatever happened to civil society? Excited discussions linking civil society to everything from democratisation to meeting basic needs seem to have gone quiet. We want to raise the debate around civil society once more. In this book, we argue that civil society is central to development for the individual citizen, collective life, and the state itself. We also believe that civil society means much more than just the aid industry. Broader concepts of civil society and its role contain the potential to create real change within the development sector. The aid industry needs the courage to be different, and ideas contained within a stronger understanding of civil society can reinvigorate our approach towards development.

By civil society, we mean the various citizen associations of all different shapes and sizes, which are neither the family unit, nor the state, nor the private sector. This can be described as the space or arena between the state and the market. This is of course extremely broad, both as a concept and in reality, but one of the points we discuss throughout this book is that the diversity, and the multiple roles of various associations in civil society is precisely what makes it important for sustainable human development.

There have been some positive indications that large development actors understand the importance of civil society in what are now considered important and legitimate development activities; such as the rise of advocacy, monitoring the state, developing people's membership groups and movements. Civil society is recognised and its importance eloquently described in the policies of most large bilateral and multilateral donors. However, in practice, models used in the aid industry and by states for the most part seem to still regard civil society as merely a link in the aid chain rather than as a core element of society and polity that is necessary for any development to take root.

Using practical case studies, which emerged from an INTRAC conference held in 2008, this book aims to develop a clearer understanding of the nature and role of civil society, prove that civil society is indeed alive and kicking, and make recommendations for more effective civil society strengthening. This volume is intended for NGOs, think tanks, multilateral and bilateral donors; all those engaged in supporting civil society, running civil society programmes, or undertaking wider programmes such as state building where it is important to take into account civil society. If the book proves useful to a greater range of civil society groups we will feel that we have contributed something worthwhile to the process of revaluing civil society.

Civil society and the aid industry

The idea of civil society was first embraced by the aid industry in the 1980s, providing a rationale and goal to support transitional states moving towards democracy, whether in the former Soviet Union or post-colonial African states. This approach to strengthening civil society was centred on the idea of societal and political transition. However, our current approach to civil society strengthening seems to have slipped into acting as if support to any NGO automatically supports civil society. Yet we know that this approach often focuses on direct poverty reduction, without integrating an understanding of how to tackle deep-rooted inequalities which serve to entrench poverty.

Those in the aid industry need to be reminded of the paramount need for longer term investment in an independent, diverse and strong civil society. If 'development assistance' does not take into account long-term, sustainable and balanced transformation, through strengthening civil society or through local capacity development, then poverty will not be eliminated in the long term, and the developmental aspect of the assistance is questionable. Similarly, too much 'development' and civil society work has been lost in the minutiae of short-term results and activities, and a deeper understanding of civil society brings into focus the less measurable, but essential, factors which build sustainable development.

Looking beyond NGOs

Influential development actors repeatedly assure us that they recognise civil society is not synonymous with NGOs. The policies of major bilateral and multilateral donors express laudable aims regarding supporting civil society. Despite this, aid agencies, and increasingly local government, do not have mechanisms to make real their rhetoric of supporting a diverse range of civil society associations that have visions which don't neatly fit into the current overarching goals of the aid architecture.[i] This tendency compounds a general lack of a shared understanding of civil society, which hinders productive debate.

If many agencies tell us they recognise that NGOs are not synonymous with civil society, why do they continue to work as though they are? One of the central themes of this book is that civil society is, and must, go 'beyond NGOs'. Whilst there has been some recognition at the level of principle that civil society essentially resides in associations of a wide variety of types, ranging from community based organisations to mass membership associations such as trade unions, faith organisations and issue-based social movements, the reality is that NGOs dominate the funded part of the civic sector. This book aims to help development practitioners think through how they can better support diverse organisations which have the legitimacy, roots and capacity to transform their own societies. Please refer to Appendix 1 for further examples of what civil society working 'beyond NGOs' looks like.

This is not to exclude NGOs from civil society. As the cartoon below shows, NGOs have a role to play, and many of the cases in this book come from NGOs. Therefore, when we discuss organisations that work within their own local contexts, we use the term CSO as inclusive of local NGOs, as well as other associations as described above (AKDN and INTRAC, 2007).

© Linda Lönnqvist 2007

However, we will always use the term 'INGO' when referring to international NGOs, to highlight the fact that these actors owe more to external origins and impetus, in contrast to local CSOs, which whether NGOs or not, are primarily associations of citizens from the societies they are trying to transform. Whilst international INGOs may well be part of civil society in their countries of origin and may have grown from solidarity and other movements, once they are transplanted to other parts of the world their nature clearly changes into being external agents. They may in many instances act in development as not-for-profit service providers distanced from local civil society.

But this is not to say that international assistance is by nature problematic. Our emphasis on local roots does not imply our opposition to global engagement. Work across national borders is perhaps more important than ever, but it must be a case of international solidarity being invoked by local civil society, or through genuinely equal coalitions and partnerships of global civil society, rather than international action emanating from the powerful, which supplants the activity of local civil society. A major contribution to development practice has been the evolution of partnership policy and practice, which aims to improve mutually beneficial ways of working. INGOs should continue to draw on this body of good practice when working with civil society.[ii]

On the other hand, it is naïve to assume that all local NGOs make a positive contribution to strengthening their societies. The huge surge of funds committed to development in recent history arguably poses a challenge for the development of a healthy local civil society, in that local associations have been absorbed into, or created by, the world of international aid which often undermines their own local legitimacy. What we argue is that any form of aided and created civil society has limits, such as:

- Involvement in the international aid industry can reduce the lack of real commitment to local issues and create the ascendancy of both personal interests – in seeing NGOs as job creation – as well as an orientation towards the world of donors.

- The professionalisation of the sector has both positive and negative aspects, with the inflated nature of NGO salaries being problematic, especially where they exceed those of important public and private sector posts.

- The dependency of NGOs on funds being channelled through government can create an unwillingness to challenge entrenched authorities.

- The culture of funding for everything – from village meetings to sitting allowances for government officials – can undermine voluntarism.

Therefore, this book is not based on the idea that particular categories of NGO are 'good' or 'bad', but rather than we do not believe that the current way that international assistance works is a substitute for the type of local civil society which has genuine long-term value for combating inequality and poverty. Nor do we make the blanket assumption that all CSOs pursue the same aims or share the same values. However the book is about those particular civic actors that are committed to 'social solidarity with the people in society they serve or represent'.[1]

The five functions that we outline explore different facets of what civil society should ideally fulfil, and illustrate opportunities and challenges associated with these.

The functions of civil society

INTRAC's understanding of the nature and role of civil society has developed through a combination of looking at contemporary case studies and theoretical debates through history. The understanding of civil society that we explore in this book is all about the

---

[1] For a similar view on the roles CSOs play in international development see the CIVICUS CSO Development Effectiveness Open Forum: www.civicus.org/development-cooperation-/cso-development-effectiveness-open-forum

role of civil society within society as a whole, in particular how it interacts with the state. The scope of this book does not extend to a full examination of civil society's interactions with the market or the family, but these are mentioned through the book, and we point to some further directions for understanding these relationships in the concluding chapter.

By asking questions about the wider role of civil society, our focus shifts away from a focus on the 'activity' level of what civil society does on a daily basis. This is important, because so much attention and concern lies at this level, examining what civil society delivers to the aid industry rather than how far civil society is contributing to local and national socio-political development. Whilst we wish to applaud the immense value of service provision and advocacy as outcomes of civil society activity, when this becomes our sole focus, it can restrict the development of the long-term benefits that are contained in broader visions of what civil society should be, which have the potential to achieve fundamental and sustainable change. As argued by a recent report on civil society in the UK and Ireland, sponsored by the Carnegie UK Trust, 'we need to set our sights far beyond narrow arguments about contracts or fiscal treatment for the voluntary sector, and look instead at how civil society activity can shape our world and how we can make a transition from an age of me to an age of we'.[iii] Most attempts to categorise civil society start by listing the types of organisation, or alternatively list the activities civil society groups carry out: supply water, rural development etc.[2]

In a world rife with internal conflict and where marked inequalities exist, we need to lift the aims of civil society strengthening up and above the activities that civil society fulfils, however important they might be. Instead we should look at how civil society can contribute to the looming questions of governance, equity, democracy, building social trust, and reducing the seeds of conflict and violence. It is clear that the battle to reduce poverty will not be won by merely technical inputs or financial flows without developing a supportive civil society which can act to demand rights, transparency and good governance from the state, and to counterbalance elite controls of the economy and polity. On this basis, we explore civil society as defined by five functions it fulfils, to:[3]

1) help generate the social basis for democracy
2) promote political accountability
3) produce social trust, reciprocity and networks
4) create and promote alternatives
5) support the rights of citizens and the concept of citizenship.

As the core of this book addresses the relationship between civil society and the state, it is important to make a distinction here between what we refer to as politics with a 'big P' as opposed to politics with a 'small p'. 'Big P' politics relates to the attempts of groups,

---
[2] See Appendix 2
[3] Most attempts to categorise civil society start by listing the types of organisation, or alternatively list the activities civil society groups carry out.

primarily political parties, to gain control of the state through political processes – whether elections or less democratic methods of dominance and control. 'Small p' politics relates to the constant negotiations between groups over priorities, resources, policies, which all of us engage in on a daily basis. It can include lobbying local or national government, and is about influencing the state in the interests of groups of citizens rather than gaining control over the state. Thus when we talk of promoting political accountability we refer to 'small p' political accountability, for example work that aims to give women fuller citizenship rights, or tackles exclusion from policy and decision making. This notion does admittedly lead to more of a focus in this book on the state–civil society relationship than a focus on civil society's work in promoting accountability in the private sector.

We do not claim that the five functions are a universal definition but feel that they highlight important aspects of the roles civil society plays which must be more clearly understood. Recent work by others complements this framework. It is interesting to note that the conclusions of the Development Research Centre on 'Citizenship, Participation and Accountability', after 10 years and many case studies, comes up with a similar framework.[iv] They identify four key democratic and developmental outcomes: 'construction of citizenship' (similar to 'supporting the rights of citizens and the concept of citizenship'); 'strengthening the practice of participation' (similar to 'building the social basis for democracy'); 'strengthening of responsive and accountable states' (similar to 'promoting political accountability'); and 'development of inclusive and cohesive society' (similar to 'producing trust, reciprocity and networks'). What they miss is our fourth function: 'creating and promoting alternatives'. But the coincidence of ideas from two very different starting points reinforces our belief that the framework of this book captures key facets of how to work towards improved governance, citizenship, and a truly developmental state.

The book will take each of the five functions as the basis for a chapter of discussion and case studies. We must clarify here that these functions are not completely separate and do not occur in isolation. Rather they are different facets of what civil society does, with overlapping elements in reality. Therefore the cases which we outline are explored under the function they best exemplify, but also may reflect several functions at a time.

The relationship between state and civil society

To understand why civil society's functions are central to effective development involves insight into the relationship between civil society and the state. Civil society works with the state to provide citizens with basic services and guarantees such as security, education, health, as well as predictable environments for commercial and social life to take place. What is more, the ability of the state to meet the needs and demands of citizens will be integrally linked to the ability of civil society to reflect the voice of citizens, through action and opinion.

Therefore, we see civil society as the context and substance from which a healthy state develops and emerges. This is the case regardless of whether the country or region is rich, middle-income or poor. Without a strong civil society, we believe that a state is unlikely to be able to tackle poverty in a sustainable way, or produce effective public goods, even where resources are not a constraint. Historically, it has been the case that weak and fragile states require a strong civil society in order to progress, as much as civil society requires a viable state in order to flourish. There is of course an ongoing debate about countries which seem to be illustrating their ability to maintain high rates of economic growth whilst keeping close control of basic freedoms, such as freedom of the press and freedom of association, and by implication the ability of an independent civil society to flourish. In particular, the surge forward of China is an attractive model for those countries wishing to maintain repressive regimes. The longer term perspective is still unknown and history seems to indicate that it is difficult to maintain such strict control over a population for very long. Arguably, the opening up of China to the private sector is the first stage of what may later be an opening up to its own citizens and civil society organisations. It remains to be seen whether as people create greater financial wealth they will then start to argue for more political and associational freedoms.

Our view is that, whether a given development project aims to reduce poverty, realise rights, or improve equity, the symbiotic relationship between civil society and state must necessarily underpin any sustainable intervention. This relationship between state and civil society is illustrated in the diagram below.

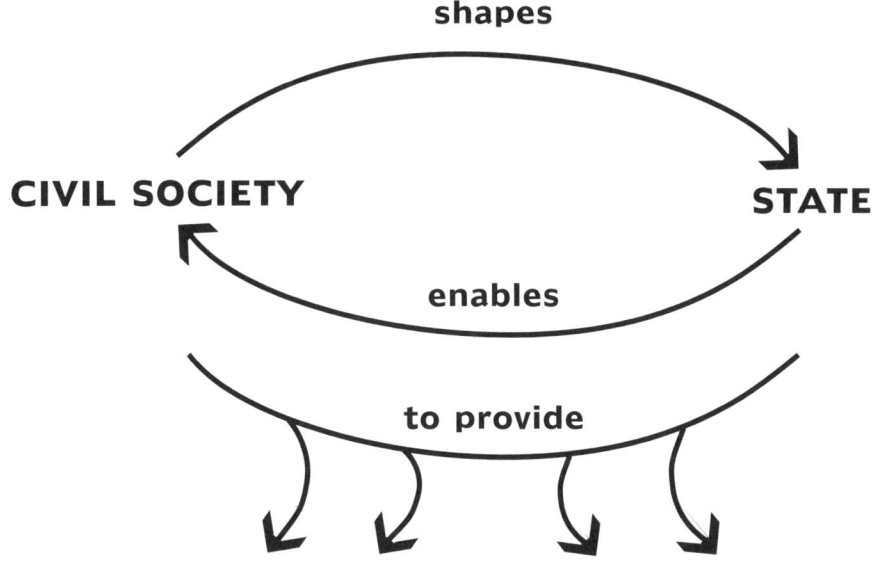

It is essential to understand that for civil society to fulfil its role, and the functions we explore in this book, it must be independent from both the state, and that other vast area of social and political life, the market. Many of the problems with the aid chain that we have so far described stem from civil society having been 'marketed' as a new commodity, or being made subservient to the state and its aims. By 'marketing' we refer to a set of factors that have led civil society groups, particularly NGOs, away from their voluntary roots towards being a part of the not-for-profit commercial sector in the way they sell products to seek funds for their own survival. Commercial techniques have taken many groups a long way from their membership and voluntary origins. The state in turn, reacting to public sector inefficiency, has channelled huge amounts of funding through NGOs as 'worthy', honest and efficient delivers of services. But this easily leads to projects initiated or heavily influenced by the state, as opposed to a voluntary sector occasionally helped through grants from public or private sources. Thus the very values and strengths of civil society that made it attractive to these sectors are now threatened by civil society's lack of independence from them. So how does civil society provide an alternative to the status quo of development assistance, whilst still being entangled in these problems?

Civil society strengthening as essential for effective development

Civil society strengthening is essential to a more holistic approach to development. Where the majority of aid flows from state to state, the small amount that goes to work with civil society is not always well spent. It would seem that much goes to NGOs simply carrying out activities from the current menu of development aid approaches. Channelling money through INGOs and their partners does not automatically strengthen civil society. Rather, a specifically civil society strengthening approach is explicitly centred around:

- A strong concept of development as a process not merely a set of deliverables

- Focus on longer term sustainable structural transformation rather than short-term results

- Supporting initiatives that come from the local society, thereby ensuring local legitimacy, rather than the isolation from local society that characterises some development aid

- Accountability to society rather than donors

- Works through being embedded in the polity (state system) rather than avoiding the political

- An emphasis on diverse approaches

- Bringing citizen and state together.

These principles highlight that civil society is not **just** a mechanism to provide services to its members. It often does so as one of the benefits of associational life, but it is not civil society's sole purpose. Of course many membership groups will seek to provide services to their members, but this is very distinct from generalist NGOs providing services through contracts with donors or local government. This is a valid position, especially in emergencies, but it often has limited value in terms of strengthening the role of citizens and civil society in the long term. There is a danger that aid industry approaches to working with civil society sanitise and depoliticise civil society, and indeed aid itself, by using civil society as a 'technical arm' in support of the MDGs or other pillars of the aid architecture.[v] Through re-orienting our perspectives to the functions of civil society set out here, we hope to enable organisations to take the most appropriate and effective longer term approaches for civil society.

But equally, international donors can easily fall into doctrinaire interpretations of strengthening civil society for 'democratisation', and can push the advocacy and watchdog functions of civil society so much as to be counterproductive. Service provision and poverty reduction may be an essential part of building a social base for democracy, although the short-term gains from these activities must always be accompanied by long-term focus on civil society, rights and citizenship. Strengthening civil society will reduce poverty and inequality in a sustainable manner through providing the locally embedded structures, competencies and state-citizen balance required for sustainable and equitable development. In the table below, we set out what we consider some of the key distinctions between the development aid and civil society strengthening perspectives.

Development aid and civil society strengthening perspectives

	Development aid perspective	Civil society strengthening perspective
Historical origins	Developed after World War 2 as decolonisation occurred. Then expanded to other developing countries.	Derived from political theory on the citizen-state relationship, particularly from the 17th century on.
Ultimate aims	Poverty alleviation and socio-economic development, more recently with increased emphasis on rights.	A strong civil society – organised citizens not part of the state, private sector or family – which is conducive to strengthened democracy, greater accountability and better governance, which in turn should reduce poverty and gross inequalities.
Geographical focus	Less developed countries, typically tropical countries, recently decolonised.	All countries, but particular emphasis on those where civil society is emergent, weak and under pressure.
Role of civil society	Optional – much development aid has focused exclusively on the state and private sector. Civil society role embraced in late 80s, given perceived limitations of other approaches.	Central, with the value of civil society being seen as intrinsic, not just instrumental. In other words civil society, as much broader than development NGOs, is recognised as a 'good' in its own right.

Poverty focus	Central, with target countries frequently dropped as they become 'better off'.	A stronger civil society may strengthen poverty reduction efforts, but affects political and social dimensions too. Civil society strengthening may be required in better off countries as well.
Political dimension	Much of development aid has been apolitical, although increased emphasis on governance and policy influencing recently.	Strengthening the political dimension – in terms of how citizens organise and relate to the state and other institutions – has always been central.
Role of official aid	Official aid has typically constituted the vast majority of development aid and tends to channel efforts to the latest aid goals.	Most civil societies predated official aid and continue without government funding.
Measuring success	Through measurements of poverty and development at the community level and progress towards goals such as the MDGs at the macro level.	Various mapping and capacity assessment tools can be used to judge the ability of the citizen and CSOs to dialogue, obtain policy changes and concessions from the state, and develop relationships outside of the immediate family.[4]

This table looks at two 'ideal' ends of a spectrum, whilst in reality there are many approaches which sit somewhere between 'development assistance' and 'civil society strengthening', but we believe that taking a step back and looking at this level, and at the functions that civil society should fulfil (illustrated by case studies) has the potential to refresh our approaches.

The ultimate aim of civil society strengthening is to move towards a sustainable and autonomous civil society that absorbs its own costs through voluntary contributions of time, expertise and funds. Getting to this ideal requires capacity building, various dimensions of which are mentioned throughout the book, although other INTRAC publications address it in detail.[5] Our focus here is more on the *ends* of the function that civil society should fulfil, although this focus should not detract from the *means* of getting there by building healthy organisations. The fact that our ultimate aim is clarifying civil society's basic functions also prompts us to stress that the distinction we make is not a simple dichotomy between INGO

---

[4] The Civil Society Index is a good example for practitioners. See: www.civicus.org/csi

[5] For further reading on capacity building, see, for example: Lipson, B. & Hunt, M. (2008) Capacity Building Framework: A values-based programming guide, Oxford: INTRAC; James, R. & Hailey, J. (2007) Capacity Building for NGOs: Making it Work, Oxford: INTRAC; James, R. (2002) People and Change: Exploring Capacity Building in NGOs, Oxford: INTRAC; James, R. (ed) (2001) Power and Partnership? Experiences of NGO Capacity Building, Oxford: INTRAC; James, R. (1998) Demystifying Organisation Development: Practical Capacity Building Experiences from African NGOs, Oxford: INTRAC.

and local CSO, North and South. There are several good examples of INGO support and action in this book. What we argue is that whilst the transfer of ideas is not bad, the imposition of them is.

Overview of the book

Having set out what we mean by civil society and why it is worthy of attention, the functions it fulfils beyond the aid chain, and why we think that strengthening an autonomous civil society is essential for effective development, including the reduction of poverty, we now turn to give a brief overview of what the rest of the book will cover.

The next five chapters will explore each of the functions which we believe capture the wider purposes, strengths and potential of civil society, and provide case studies of how these purposes have been realised in practice worldwide. In each of these chapters, we start by describing the essence of the function in question, and provide a short summary of the key theoretical ideas behind each function. For those interested in the theoretical development of the concept of civil society, Appendix 2 includes more detail.[6] Each chapter consists of case studies, and ends with recommendations that have arisen from the cases, and a summary of key learning points. It is obviously not possible to document the full range of civil society ideas and actions relevant to each function. As we have already mentioned, the functions we explore relate more closely to civil society's relations with the state than with the market. But in each chapter we have attempted to capture the character of the wide range of civil society initiatives working to fulfil that function. We include both impressive and innovative examples and others which illustrate continuing challenges.

Chapter 2 explores how civil society helps **generate the social basis for democracy**. The culture of democracy starts from the way a small village association is run and spreads through collective activity all the way up to processes such as general elections. The experience of negotiating between positions, opinions, and interests at a local level and participation in civic life can extend democracy both amongst the grass roots, and up to the national level, especially in terms of promoting multiple, often minority, interests in relation to the majority political system. For example, members' involvement in trade unions strengthens these organisations to interact with other parts of civil society and the state, influencing and making decisions that reflect multiple interests. Through the case studies we explore how both service provision and advocacy activities can help build the social basis for democracy, and should be seen as interlinked. The cases also illustrate how in order for associational life to build the culture of democracy, civil society organisations need to draw upon their own traditions of connecting with citizens and building networks with one another.

---

[6] Civil society has been understood through history in very different ways and these can lead to very different political outcomes. Although in the aid industry we often discuss civil society as a new concept, traced to the process which brought down the Iron Curtain, it is far older in terms of the underlying political philosophy, and the rich and long history of people organising collectively beyond state structures. Appendix 2 explores some of these historical developments, giving the background to some of the positions we take in this book.

Although externally designed programmes can play an enabling role, the impetus and power to drive social change should come from within civil society. This is particularly important when considering who has the mandate and authority to act as a watchdog to government.[7]

Chapter 3 looks at how civil society **promotes political accountability beyond party politics**. Local level monitoring of diverse causes by groups with particular interests provides a counter balance to restricted, elite control. From the small scale acceptance of the fact that each citizen has the right to speak, through to the concept that political leaders have responsibility to their fellow citizens, political accountability is built up through a myriad of relationships and experiences. The cases illustrate how broad-based solidarity and South–South cooperation are powerful bases for action. Such action can work internationally to impact the global human rights architecture, and in turn, slowly improve the political accountability of repressive regimes. Several of the cases also testify to the positive role of the media in civil society efforts to promote political accountability, and how civil society can use this as part of their efforts to make changes at the legal and institutional level effective within a society. The chapter ends by exploring how relationships between different actors are necessary to open up civic space and channels to demand political accountability; and suggests that northern NGOs may sometimes need to learn when to step back if they are to really strengthen this local capacity.

Chapter 4 looks at how civil society **produces social trust, reciprocity and networks**. Civic community in the form of horizontal organisations such as unions, sports clubs, parent–teacher associations and religious communities build up what some call 'social capital' – which creates the environment for transactions to take place, based on the trust that they will be honoured. The cases here explore the different roles played by social capital under a variety of governance conditions. In situations of injustice, the cases demonstrate the power of membership organisations reliant on solidarity between the oppressed to act effectively for change in society. In fragile democracies, building horizontal networks in civil society, facilitated by new technology, can develop relational capacities that last beyond specific campaigns, and may later transform into political capacities. In contexts where trust and transparency are sorely lacking, working slowly and painstakingly towards a participatory basis for civil rather than conflictual interaction with entrenched authorities is challenging, but essential.

Chapter 5 looks at how civil society **creates and promotes alternatives** through collective action, whether at the level of ideas or in practice. New concepts, activities, institutions and socio-economic solutions often arise through civil society, from the communal to the international level. Innovations in the case studies range from creating alternatives to problematic power relations in land ownership, public housing, and agricultural knowledge. This freedom to evolve ideas within civil society also presents challenges, in that ideas require negotiation and a struggle for legitimacy across and within civil society as well as with the state and market. This chapter illustrates solutions that overlap with the other functions of

---

[7] More material can be found via the work of the 'Citizenship, Partnership and Accountability' Development Research Centre at IDS Sussex: www.drc-citizenship.org

civil society, but particularly highlights the important role of civil society in tackling the status quo power relations, and the need for those working in and with civil society to have the courage and determination to risk testing different ideas to come up with the most effective solution.

Chapter 6 discusses civil society's function to **support the rights of citizens and the concept of citizenship**. The idea of a contract between state and citizen is much older than the recent emphasis on 'rights-based approaches'. The state earns and retains its legitimacy through fulfilling certain obligations to its citizens, and in turn, people within a society take active citizenship by engaging the state and lobbying for specific interests, rights, services and protections. The case studies in this chapter look at some of the challenges associated with supporting civil society's function to promote active citizenship. Civil society must be alert to governments that see no benefit in an autonomous civic arena, and that gradually undermine the rights of its citizens. There are many challenges around supporting marginalised groups of citizens. Interventions may be based on merely 'inviting' these groups to participate in shaping policy, rather than trying to support citizens' capacity to create spaces based in collective identity, which then drive activism and genuine calls for civil rights. Equally, programming for 'strong publics' should not take a one-size-fits-all approach but think about how to promote engagement across various parts of civil society which may be disparate and have very different priorities.

Finally, Chapter 7 summarises the key points that have emerged from looking at the case studies of civil society's strengths and weaknesses on the ground. These recommendations are useful to those interested in working with civil society groups, either in designing civil society support programmes, funding civil society, or looking at how their other programmes may help or hinder the long-term development of a healthy civil society and, in the process, healthy human development. Not all NGO work with civil society necessarily strengthens civil society, especially in the context of international assistance driven by specific and often short-term targets. Whilst market forces have propelled INGO activity forward, they have also weakened many other CSOs' capacities to evolve their own programmes and respond to the inevitable needs for change in their societies from the bottom up and inside out. Even in the developed world civil society has been under pressure, as summarised in a recent report on civil society in the UK: 'For a century or more it has been pushed to the margins by commerce and the state, which have claimed the lion's share of resources and power.'[vi]

We recommend that a healthy civil society strengthening strategy should include: a strong emphasis on building networks and coalitions across civil society associations of all different shapes and sizes; placing a high value on membership based groups; a focus on the enabling environment, with institutional support for civil society legally, in government policy, and public understanding; long-term capacity building of the competencies of people and organisations; and finally, making a dedicated effort to build towards strong, diverse, and sustainable civil society. These pointers encourage us to turn the tables, and let civil society shape our development agendas once again.

2

Building the social basis for democracy

Introduction

Civil society extends a culture of democracy from the grassroots upwards. It does this by protecting and representing multiple interests, often those of minorities, against majority rule. This function of civil society goes well beyond the 'free and fair' elections that have been the emphasis of so much of the democratisation agenda in the last few decades. Rather, through civic participation, from a small local sports group to national-level movements, the culture of democracy is created. The experience at the local level of democratic ways of working – negotiating between interests, compromising, and taking larger perspectives in participatory organisations – creates norms, systems and networks that form the basis for democracy at the national level.

> **Theoretical background**
>
> The idea of civil society can be traced back to the writings of Cicero in the first century BC, who identified it as the domain of public activity separate from private and domestic life. Civil society was constituted by the elite males of a city-state acting in their role of responsible publicly minded citizens, deliberating upon how they should be governed and who should govern. It did not exist in opposition to the state; rather, the state was seen to be an instrument of civil society.[vii] John Locke brought the concept into the modern age. He described civil society as the realm of political association wherein people leave the chaotic 'state of nature' and enter into a commonwealth with a common law and authority. To enter into civil society requires each member to submit themselves to a shared public authority. For both Cicero and Locke, to participate in civil society is to deliberate about matters of public interest and the way in which people ought to be governed. They saw civil society as the social matrix of the democratic state. Civil society is the context and substance from which a democratic state develops and emerges. Equally, the mere existence of multiple organisations is not what strengthens democracy; it is the way in which these organisations promote active participation that really matters.[viii]

A state without a strong civil society is an exercise of absolute power. This leads to totalitarian states and poor conditions for human development. The cases demonstrate how civil society has contributed to building a democratic culture, showing CSOs which are carving out the space to associate in pursuit of their members' collective interests and democratic ideals, often in the face of weak, unresponsive, competitive, even repressive states. The variety of examples reflect the fact that building the social basis of democracy involves taking into account the diverse realities of what is effective and necessary on the ground in different contexts. Some 'traditional' CSOs, groups or associations exist to meet the needs of members, and other 'modern' advocacy NGOs lobby the government on particular issues affecting the public's rights, such as democratic accountability. Whilst there has been criticism of groups who limit their actions to service provision, equally, international donors can easily fall into doctrinaire interpretations of what strengthening civil society looks like, and can push the advocacy and watchdog functions of civil society so much as to be counterproductive. Hence, building the social basis for democracy often involves a combination of service provision and advocacy, and networks of civil society organisations encompassing both approaches should be encouraged.

In the first case we see civil society in Kyrgyzstan challenging a new democracy which is already showing authoritarian and corrupt tendencies, by building courage to tackle governance issues.[8] At the same time, networking with both other CSOs and local authorities has been important for Kyrgyz CSOs in the absence of opportunities to influence policy at higher levels. Where expressions of civil society reside in traditional or self-help associations, emphasising participatory processes and networks can help to build these organisations' capacities.

The second case from remote Northeast India also shows civil society taking a holistic approach, combining and balancing different activities to build democracy. Civil society and its associational principles exist in diverse settings, and here civil society is beginning to recreate itself by bridging the extremes of high-profile activism in state capitals, and values-based services in remote areas, in a new generation of CSOs. These recognise that building a democratic culture starts at the grass roots, often at a very basic level, with long-term solidarity. Advocacy has little place unless accompanied by effective, concrete service delivery that builds social cohesion amongst disparate communities.

The cases from Paraguay and Ethiopia emphasise that building the social basis for democracy is not amenable to artificial creation, but is only effective when it is embedded in local associational and civic life. In Paraguay, a bilateral aid programme aimed to build the country's tenuous democracy, and the case grapples with the issues around large scale funding and external donor-led civil society strengthening. Building the capacity of a large number of CSOs had positive impacts and created activity, but questions remain around civil society's ability within such programmes to strengthen democracy through their own agendas, and capacity to continue their work when funding cycles come to an end. The Ethiopian

---

[8] Since this case study was written, the Kyrgyz government was overthrown in April 2010, and the new President guaranteed a less authoritarian governance approach for the future. The relationship between civil society and the state in Kyrgyzstan is still in flux.

case also provides a note of caution against the international community's instrumental approach to encouraging civil society to act as a watchdog, this time for aid disbursements through government. Moreover, the highly charged 2005 election, which produced an unexpectedly good showing for the opposition, convinced the government that the international community was steering the advocacy work of local civil society in a new era of aid conditionality based on a western democratisation agenda. The immediate effect was a clampdown on 'political' civil society that put paid to years of donor preparations for launching harmonised aid to the government, and the longer term result came in 2008 with a revised civil society law that effectively constrained advocacy by any CSO that depends upon foreign funding.

Case studies

2.1 Building the social basis of democracy in Kyrgyzstan

In new democracies, citizens and activists often have high expectations of a sea change in relations between the citizen and the state. When governments fail to embrace the new democratic culture, CSOs can become forceful opponents. However, CSOs are also compelled to adapt to a variety of circumstances, and networking and alliance building is important, building the social basis of democracy both within civil society and between CSOs and local authorities.

Transition from centrally planned communist rule to market-orientated democracies has failed so far to improve governance and popular participation in many of the Central Asian states. Kyrgyzstan, a mountainous country in the heart of Central Asia with a population of five million, is one of the poorest of the former Soviet Republics. After the break-up of the Soviet Union its transition was initially full of promise compared to its neighbours. But persistent poverty and growing inequality combined with corruption, inefficiency and vote rigging provoked the so called 'Tulip Revolution' and an ensuing regime change in 2005. The parliament grew weaker and the President stronger. Civil society found it difficult to demand greater accountability from government, and NGOs that depended on external funding were vulnerable to charges of being manipulated by foreign interests. In this challenging context there were a number of strategies that civil society used. One of these has been a move from service provision to activism on governance issues, and another a greater emphasis on networking with one another and local authorities.

Since this case was originally written, the importance of CSOs in strengthening the social basis for democracy across ethnic lines was bought into sharp relief in 2010 by the dismissed Kyrgyz government's scapegoating of the Uzbek minority. The tragic outcome highlights the need in multi-ethnic states of inclusive associations and other CSOs that bring together rather than segregate different ethnicities and clans. Whilst the case reflects the relationships between state and civil society in Kyrgyzstan before April 2010, many of these dynamics will continue to be relevant both in Kyrgyzstan and elsewhere.

Moving towards activism for democratic governance

Although Kyrgyz NGOs only appeared as civil society actors in the early 1990s, they evolved rapidly. Whilst initially they were addressing the social problems of transition purely as service providers in the context of a breakdown of state-based services, soon they were complementing the work of authorities and gradually moved on to negotiating space and service agreements at local levels. However, the new millennium brought the realisation that service provision on its own could only mitigate, and not resolve the many social problems of transition. NGO activists familiar with advocacy experimented with a more political approach. They tapped into their own societies' traditions of civil activism, home-grown movements for solutions to local problems, and built alliances to influence decision making. Some have recently started forging relationships with like-minded political parties that shared their values of justice, democratisation and fairness in governance.

For example, through the 1990s the Centre InterBilim was a typical Bishkek development NGO implementing a range of social programmes. But it started to adopt an overtly political stance and by 2005 along with other Kyrgyz NGOs began campaigning for change. After the rigged elections of the following year a coalition of NGOs called a demonstration against the government and mobilised a movement to reform the constitution. By 2008 the movement that it mobilised had installed a 'Public Parliament' in parallel with the existing and highly problematic ruling body. Progressive forces have been brought together by these actions, but InterBilim has bemoaned the lack of courage of international partners that are fearful of funding overtly political action by NGOs.

Networking with other civil society actors and local authorities

Whilst some like InterBilim identified more clearly an activist and advocacy role and attitude towards government, others took a less confrontational role. In an environment where there is little trust in society and NGOs are suspected of working to a foreign agenda, traditional forms of networking have made a real contribution to building relationships of partnership and negotiation that should contribute to building the social basis of democracy in the long term.

A more direct approach to the government using advocacy and campaigning was often difficult, given the lack of influence citizens had over policy makers and a government which remained unaccountable. The government was also often suspicious of NGOs and largely considered *non*-governmental activity as *anti*-governmental because of its perceived dependence on foreign funding. 'Policy intervention' was generally understood by the government as threatening demands for 'political change'. There were, for instance, no official platforms for policy dialogue with authorities at the national level and so no forum for discussing issues of joint interest such as the country development strategy, or social contracting by the state.

The Dutch INGO ICCO has funded work exploring the potential for more impact from networking between its local partners. They all work for the social mobilisation of the 'new poor' created by transition, using methods based on the Indian model of self-help groups (SHG), which they integrate with Ashar, the traditional Kyrgyz institution for reciprocity.[9] This

---

[9] Self-help groups are groups of 10-12 people (usually women) who meet each week to mobilise savings and discuss their plans.

work showed that on the one hand networking with local authorities seems to be giving civil society greater space and success at the local level, on the other hand Kyrgyz CSOs greatly need to continue to build networks 'downwards' and horizontally at the grassroots.

They found that for Kyrgyz CSOs networking and partnering with councils and other local bodies has provided a smoother route to increasing the impact of their work. These partnerships depend mostly on the goodwill and personal relations established with individual local officials. One example of using networking to increase effectiveness is Mekhr Shavkat, a large NGO operating in the agricultural belt of the Ferghana Valley. To resolve local issues such as lack of roads and power it networks with the local authorities, gaining a degree of policy influence and oversight of the budget. At the regional level it shares experience of community engagement in water and sanitation, gaining expertise and contacts that lead to projects and funding to promote water committees and local water infrastructure projects. In order to lobby ministries more effectively for better terms in joint projects, Mekhr Shavkat also networks with three peer NGOs in the Ferghana Valley.

However, ICCO's survey also found a great need for Kyrgyz NGOs to improve networking with their constituency, as the relationship is more often patron-client in style than egalitarian. Although NGOs accept the responsibility to support their constituencies' rights and needs, in building social democracy, Kyrgyz civil society needs to continue to improve its own democratic credentials through taking participatory approaches and their stakeholders seriously. One way of doing this would be to build on the informal, traditional institutions such as the Mahallya, the lowest level of the administration, the Ashar principle of reciprocal labour, or the traditional Aksakal courts which are still effective for solving day-to-day problems in rural Kyrgyz communities. Such informal links and associations based in clan, family or religious communities frequently have greater significance for people than more distant, formal and political connections.

The trust potential of such traditional forms of networking seem an effective counterbalance to the problems of Kyrgyzstan's third sector, where only around 500 of the 8,000 registered public organisations are actually active. This is due to the imported character of development, the inheritance of a paternalistic Soviet psychology, financial and programmatic dependence on donors, and weak management and communication with stakeholders.

Lessons

In challenging contexts where the state is unaccountable, civil society often takes a variety of approaches. Building the social basis of democracy in Kyrgyzstan has involved both oppositional and partnership roles for civil society in relation to the state. Some have moved from service provision toward political activism in order to tackle the background factors causing poverty. Political activism is a legitimate role of civil society. No one argues, for instance, that civil society should not have lined up behind the ANC in its struggle against apartheid. However, how best to engage with a politically active civil society is one of the continual struggles for donors. This case has shown that capacity building of CSOs such as InterBilim is one solution as, over time, this capacity has been passed on to opposition parties, hopefully resulting in improvements to the political space, a fundamental task for civil society. Yet sluggish and inequitable transitions are failing to arrest the decline of peoples' living conditions in Central Asia. This inevitably exacerbates the challenges around trust faced by local NGOs that are dependent on international resources. In these circumstances local civil society has to look inside its own traditions to find legitimacy, through building informal networks with local authorities, and by continuing to work towards strengthening accountability to its constituents.

2.2 Combining service delivery and advocacy in India's northeast

The landlocked and isolated Northeastern region of India has seven states that border Bangladesh, Bhutan, Burma and Tibet along 5,000km of porous frontiers.[10] The region is plagued by recurring armed conflicts over ethnicity and identity issues, numerous insurgent groups, acute poverty and crippled governance. In combination, these facts are major constraints to development and deny citizens the fruits of democracy, peace and a thriving civil society.

The key question for civil society is: can it respond to so many democratic deficits and if so, how can it do that? This case suggests that the answer is not through a single method, but rather CSOs possess attributes that help to build social democracy in different ways and in different measures. Sometimes CSOs need to embrace new, and broader, ways of working to stimulate the culture of democracy. In the Northeast advocacy and service delivery organisations are discovering the benefits of combining their approaches.

Many of the social movements of the Northeast are ethnically nationalist and distinctly uncivil in their effects. Even so, within the small communities of the region, there has traditionally been a great deal of trust and solidarity. Varied forms of informal networks and associational life reinforce trust around cultural traditions and festivities. Slowly but surely, this social capital is transforming into more organised forms of engagement in the wider community in which concerned citizens can engage themselves in constructive work to build the social basis for democracy.

The civil sector revolves traditionally around two main sets of actors, from both inside and outside the region. The 'insiders' are urban-based professionals, often student activists who are deeply engaged in the region's politics. They see their primary function as advocating for the political interests of particular communities. Professional NGOs led by 'insiders' have mushroomed in recent years in response to the availability of international donor funds. However, the sector is not stable and leaders often leave to join political parties. The 'outsiders' are followers of Gandhi who three decades ago dispersed across India to set up village-level NGOs, often in very isolated locations. Their grassroots activities focus on improving living conditions and services as well as reducing communal violence through Gandhian methods of civil disobedience, pursuit of truth and non-violence. Their work is

---

[10] Known collectively as the 'Seven Sister States' because they are so isolated and inter-dependent, they are: Arunachal Pradesh, Assam, Manipur, Meghalaya, Mizoram, Nagaland and Tripura. They account for four per cent of India's population – approximately 41 million people.

much appreciated by the villagers, but it is too dispersed to make an impact at any level beyond the immediate locality.

There has traditionally been little communication between insiders and outsiders. Government remains aloof from both, regarding service provision as its own preserve despite a poor record, and being unresponsive to calls for improved human rights or good governance. There are few international donors, owing partly to restrictions in this sensitive frontier zone. However civil society is beginning to resolve old divisions. A new generation of young activists has emerged which has learned to combine rights-based advocacy with practical activities, and engage the government constructively by demonstrating innovations that work. The following organisations illustrate this point while representing the 'insider' and 'outsider' traditions:

The Chakma Students Union (CSU)

Some 'insider' organisations, whilst remaining committed to their work on empowerment and entitlements, are at the same time finding ways of complementing the state's service provision function. In recent years the CSU has spearheaded a movement for social and political rights, particularly citizenship, for the Chakmas, an ethnic group living in the state of Arunachal Pradesh since the 1960s, as these people are historically disadvantaged and face complete social and political exclusion in the state.[11] The students who had been part of the movement have now started to feel the need to add more rooted constructive work to their activism if their community's marginalisation is to be alleviated. Young lawyers and teachers started SNEHA, a not-for-profit, philanthropic organisation and under that banner opened a primary school at a remote village in Arunachal Pradesh. Within three years, the new school was offering education to more than 400 children, first generation learners whose parents are illiterate, landless labourers living in extreme poverty.

© Linda Lönnqvist 2008. www.developmentcartoons.com

---

[11] The Chakma are amongst 100,000 Bangladeshi tribal people who were displaced by construction of the massive Kaptai damn in 1962. Few ever received adequate compensation and 60,000 sought refuge across the border. Their status as Indian citizens was finally made possible by the Indira-Mujib Pact of 1972, but much remains to be done to implement the letter and spirit of the agreement.

Tamulpur Anchalik Gramdan Sangh (TAGS)
There is potential for those associational forms of civil society that are grounded in needs-driven, practical work, to evolve further to transform conflict situations and political tensions. TAGS is a Gandhian organisation which has been working in Tamulpur block, Assam, for the last four decades. Tamulpur shares a border with Bhutan and has often been a transit point for insurgents to cross over to the neighbouring kingdom. Whilst improving services through voluntarism has long been their approach, recent TAGS work has evolved to mobilise a thousand women from small towns and villages in Assam, Manipur, Tripura and Arunachal Pradesh to form the Women's Peace Brigade (*Mahila Shanti Sena*). Since its formation in these states, these women have stressed the need to build peace both in private lives and in the public domain. In a series of events over the last two years, they organised seminars, public meetings and rallies for concerned citizens. During a recent outburst of inter-ethnic violence in Assam, these young leaders displayed courage and determination. They led a peace march and kept a constant vigil around their community and neighbourhood. While they averted violence of any kind in their own area, the incident left more than 50 people dead elsewhere. From the basis of the Women's Peace Brigade, other issues have been addressed. It brought to public attention the strength of grassroots and female leaders, and these women also used the civic space they had won to negotiate for viable income generating activities and livelihood opportunities to build peace. The Department of Science and Technology under the Government of India and North Eastern Council have now come forward to support this initiative.

Lessons
To provide the social basis for democracy in volatile regions, CSOs need to combine service delivery with activism for stronger rights of the marginalised in the right proportions. Service provision and advocacy approaches are not mutually exclusive but rather mutually enriching, especially in fragile contexts. The first key lesson is that rights-based approach of empowering the community to demand better services from the state should be rooted in community work building up these minimal levels of basic entitlements. The second lesson is to pilot interventions and then lobby. Significant work with the community, whether on education, health or livelihoods, is a necessary prerequisite to making an impact upwards and engaging with authorities. Piloting a successful community based model that is facilitated by a voluntary organisation clearly demonstrates good practice in building a democratic culture. This approach is more credible than trying to train state personnel in an unproved, theoretical model.

2.3 Regime change and bilateral programming for democracy in Paraguay

Over the last decade, large-scale, multi-year civil society strengthening programmes were the stock response of bilateral donors to the many transitions from authoritarian regimes of various types to some form of democracy. Can outside interventions of any sort, let alone at this level, genuinely help build the social basis for democracy? The jury is still out on the impact of these efforts. Here we reflect on official means of strengthening civil society.

In 2008 the unlikely figure of Fernando Lugo, an ex-Bishop with leanings to Liberation Theology, succeeded in bringing to an end sixty years of one party rule in Paraguay, including 36 years of dictatorship under General Alfredo Stroessner. Local and international observers remarked on the important role played by CSOs in keeping the electoral process honest and transparent. Seven years earlier, a Paraguayan NGO, the Centre of Information and Resources for Development (CIRD), had started implementing a $6 million, USAID-funded programme 'Citizens' Initiatives'. Inevitably there was some excitement after the 2008 elections. Had this program contributed to instituting democratic practices in Paraguay by strengthening CSOs? A positive answer to this question would be welcome evidence for bilateral donors that their civil society strengthening programmes were after all able to deliver democracy.

'Citizens' Initiatives' was not conceived as a regime changing programme – it could hardly have got past the watchful Colorado Party if it had been. Rather, the theory behind it was that in order to institute democratic practices, Paraguay needed a more active civil society and that a more active civil society needed stronger CSOs. The problem was that CSOs lacked important capacities and that this inhibited or reduced citizen action on important public policies. The main objectives of the programme were: to put in place permanent mechanisms to increase citizen participation in the public decision-making process; to strengthen the capacity of CSOs to advocate for their causes; to improve their oversight of public institutions with a poor record of governance and transparency; and finally, to strengthen individual CSOs.

The first phase of the program focused on strengthening capacities in CSOs. Over five years, 2001–05, the programme offered capacity building services in a decentralised and demand-led way beyond the capital, to a coalition of CSOs such as NGOs, neighbourhood commissions, local health councils, community heath boards, and disabled peoples' organisations. Capacity building took place through financial, technical assistance and training, and networking support components. The second phase, 2006–09, moved from institutional strengthening to supporting the advocacy functions of the coalition. For the CSOs this meant promoting citizen oversight of the judiciary, citizen access to public information and support for a new national network of associations of citizen monitors. As it transpired, the main focus of the donor was on this watchdog role of civil society, given the corrupt and inefficient government. Several performance measurement tools were used to monitor impact of both capacity building and local government accountability.

Several challenges arose in what was essentially a technocratic approach to strengthening civic organisations and institutions. First, in order to build trust, CIRD was constantly adjusting the grants mechanisms for transparency and fairness especially between Asunción-based NGOs and those in the regions. Another challenge was to keep everybody accountable, which CIRD addressed by producing standard administrative procedures manuals and assigning a coach to interact with groups of CSO grantees. Measurement of capacity strengthening was also challenging, the best solution being the CSO Index applied as a self-assessment survey for organisational capacity. The most important challenge was how to change the programme's orientation and purpose when institutional strengthening was dropped and emphasis was put on concrete results for advocacy and oversight activities. CIRD managed this by replacing 'coaching' with supervision and a more results-demanding relationship with CSOs.

By 2008 the programme had reached deep into the social and administrative structures of the country. More than 220 CSOs were involved in some part of the programme, as were 150 municipal governments. CIRD feels that the programme has made an important contribution to consolidating democratic practices in Paraguay, in terms of transparency, policy influence and alliances between sectors. CIRD's attention to monitoring certainly provides evidence of a great deal of concrete activity. For example 15 advocacy coalitions started up, associated with 15 nation-wide public awareness campaigns. The programme's activities can be linked to 30 Presidential decrees and resolutions, as well as 17 municipal legislation projects. There was also substantial cross-sector cooperation, for example no less than 65 working agreements with municipal governments. This shows that the programme contributed to a positive long-term tightening of laws and regulations for better governance and more transparency within a fledgling democracy.

However, drawing causal links between a technically good programme and a nation-wide transition from one-party rule is overambitious. This project was extremely lucky in its timing as the Paraguayan people were more than ready for change. The election of the moderate Bishop almost certainly had more to do with public disgust at Colorado Party in-fighting, and the powerful popular appeal of Lugo's Liberation Theology than with the civil society strengthening programme. And there remain questions about the autonomy of the civil society organisations that were supported through the programme. Although sensitively and efficiently handled by the local implementing agency, the project still worked on the basis of contracting CSOs to fulfil specified targets.

Lessons

The Paraguay programme has undertaken a good deal of positive activity in the area of civil society strengthening. Whilst this programme strengthened organisations and helped create CSO activity, it remains a technocratic process, albeit an effective one, created externally and extended outwards and downwards from the capital. As CIRD itself points out; 'foreign funding for democracy strengthening and CSO capacity building is linked, in the mind of most people, and in reality, to foreign government interests. A common goal of democracy does not eliminate the risk of this kind of assistance being seen as an intrusion in local affairs'.[ix]

In the end the case does not lead to a simple positive or negative message about bilateral civil society strengthening programmes. Programmes like this, which stimulate an enabling environment, can professionalise the sector and boost activity and cooperation between sectors, but civil society is ultimately more than the sum total of strong CSOs. The real driver for political accountability must come from within. On rare occasions, such as in Paraguay, civil society demonstrates a strong commonality of purpose to bring about regime change. National rather than international action drove change in Serbia, when youth lead the mass uprising against Milosevic in 2000, or in the Philippines, when Marcos was overthrown. We must therefore be pragmatic in our understanding of what bilateral aid can change, and focus on supporting the wider conditions necessary for change in a society. Detailed targets derived from performance management systems are at best irrelevant to such demonstrations of civic defiance, as only outputs from prescribed activities are captured rather than their contribution to any broader social change they may or may not have generated. What is important is ensuring that external funding allows CSOs, as far as possible, to set their own agendas and make independent decisions.

2.4. Leading civil society up the governance path in Ethiopia

Building the social basis for democracy is an ambitious and complex task at the best of times. When it goes wrong it is usually because donors try to make use of civil society to their own ends or do not fully understand civil society and its complex relations with the state. This is illustrated in this case, which outlines the unanticipated fall out in 2005 in the relationship between bilateral development agencies and their 'donor darling', the Ethiopian government, just as bilaterals and multilaterals were about to move from project-based funding to direct budget support to the Ethiopian Federal Treasury.

This case has many lessons, especially about getting carried away with topical development trends, and forgetting how they can mean completely different things to different actors at different times. In this case the donor agenda of 'democratisation' and 'good governance' were pushed through a series of donor instruments at the expense of a slower, more locally rooted approach to building the social basis of democracy. Trouble was brewing from the moment the government suspected that a segment of Ethiopian civil society popular with donors and INGOs had become co-opted by the international community (and Diaspora) to drive a political agenda at the 2005 elections. It reacted as rulers in emerging democracies often do, by clamping down hard on civil society, although the full extent of its reaction was not seen for four years.

While responsibility for what followed the elections remains contested, there were demonstrations, violent repression, deaths, arrests and jail sentences. Direct budget support (DBS) was suspended as donors recoiled and the government was pilloried internationally. While DBS was replaced with a more focussed instrument for funding sub-national basic service delivery tied to a social accountability intervention with civil society, relationships remained strained. Finally, in January 2009, legislation was passed to prevent national charities and societies in receipt of more than 10% of their income from foreign sources undertaking any democratisation, advocacy, human rights or religious activity beyond service provision.

Almost two decades of communist rule under the Derg had ended in 1991 and the following year the victorious EPRDF – Ethiopian People's Revolutionary Democratic Front, set up a transitional government that put in place a decentralised, ethnically based federal structure of nine semi-autonomous regions. Periodic elections gradually gave more space to opposition parties, but the ruling style was directive and important civil rights – freedom of the press for example – were not fully enjoyed. The country was also volatile, with ethnic and regional problems amongst the traditionally marginalised Omoro and in the Ogaden – giving the government a reason to maintain what amounted to one party rule.

Civil society roles in Ethiopia

Although traditional Ethiopian civil society revolves around ethnic loyalties it also expresses itself in intense associative life at the grassroots. A large proportion of adults, men and women, keep up multiple memberships in *ekub* savings and credit schemes, the ubiquitous *iddir* funeral societies as well as the monthly 'saints' family groups and other mechanisms for citizens coming together around a common purpose. As it extends its reach this associative life naturally grows in organisational complexity and inevitably meets official structures in the form of the political and party administration, which are established from the Federal level to the smallest hamlet. Dealing with the administration while remaining independent from it requires considerable organisational skill and particular groups are not shy of co-opting officials into their own structures if they feel the need, for example, of more bargaining power to further their ends.

A more recent manifestation of Ethiopian civil society has its origins in the famine of 1984. Ethiopians engaged by international NGOs gained organisational skills by implementing large scale humanitarian programmes. As the crises receded and the new government played a more assertive role in emergency preparedness and management, these agencies shifted to longer term development and, in keeping with international trends, exposed their staff to rights-based approaches along with the associated concepts of accountability, good governance and democratisation derived from OECD norms. The apocalyptic extent of the famine meant that the scale of recruitment into this new segment of civil society was correspondingly large. Ethiopian NGOs gradually formed to provide the new sector with a variety of services, especially advocacy, which for maximum effect needed to be fronted by citizens of the country.

A good summary of the state of civil society is as follows; 'Ethiopia has a strong traditional civil society which is rooted in and resourced from local communities but not organised to engage with Government on macro issues of accountability and democratic development; and a weak modern civil society sector which comprises metropolitan elites, entirely resourced from external sources and well-connected to mechanisms for campaigning and lobbying on macro issues of accountability and democracy'.[x]

Donors and government

Not only are the two parts of civil society poorly linked, but the international donor community's interest in civil society was rarely focused upon its more 'traditional' manifestations in Ethiopia. Donors had little time to understand it and few mechanisms for engaging with it. On the other hand the metropolitan elite variety of civil society spoke a familiar language of rights, and was well linked with familiar international organisations, which could provide references if necessary. It was also at hand in the capital to network with donor officials. In short, 'modern' civil society was a useful ally in the aid industry, but most of all donor representatives needed to demonstrate to donor government head offices that local watchdogs were in place to oversee funds they were planning to disburse directly to the government budget.

As already outlined, however, this backfired. Donors were never in a position to protect the very organisations of civil society which they had drawn into the line of fire. By outlawing internationally-funded advocacy activities, the government sent a clear message that it would not allow the politicisation of Ethiopian civil society, nor would it submit to what it described as 'democratic structural adjustment', an emerging form of aid conditionality.

The argument here is not that Ethiopian CSOs should not have protested the election outcomes, but that INGOs and donors should not assume their agendas match more than a limited section of civil society's agenda. From the point of view of the aid industry, it is perhaps logical that civil society should monitor the government use of donor aid investments. But this instrumental view of civil society may be unrelated to civil society's self-concept in various countries. In Ethiopia the more politicised NGOs had a limited base of support within wider civil society, which had no expectation of immediate multi-party democracy. Especially in the countryside, civil society was engaged in organising itself at the level of solidarity groups and building these up into associations. For the Ethiopian government, the issue was that one part of civil society had crossed the line between politics with a 'small p' and with a 'big P', questioning the governing regime at the time of a contested election.

Lessons

The aid industry has an alarming tendency to believe that its own architecture for intervention in developing countries is more than just an externally-designed bureaucratic structure. To develop these structures, donors build on their own policies, strategies, and allies, often based on an imperfect understanding of the societies in question. In this case confusing the aid industry with embedded local civil society, in terms of its mandate and authority to act as a watchdog to government, led to the creation – and eventual destruction – of a segment of civil society made in the aid industry's own image. There are many lessons for all involved in this case, but the key lesson is that civil society is not the same as the aid industry.

Recommendations

The cases have shown that multiple strands of civic activity, whether contestation or service provision, can build up a culture of democracy from the grassroots. Civil society should not be boxed into the role of merely opposing the state, nor of just replacing its service provision functions. Rather, the important thing to support is the 'thickening' of civil society – more active groups and more links between different groups – whether they are coming together on one issue for a short period, or forming longer term alliances, or merely creating a critical mass of opinion and action driven by their overlapping membership bases. The following recommendations should help those who want to support civil society in its function to build the social basis of democracy.

1. Support people to learn the art of democracy from the inside out and bottom up

Negotiation between different interests, rather than simple use of power by one group over another – whether based on gender, generation, ethnicity, clan and family or political membership – is key to building democracy. To create the social basis of democracy, it is essential to build a democratic culture within CSOs as well as in wider society. Therefore the experience for citizens of working in or with a democratic organisation is almost as important as the mission of the organisation. The experiences of participating in meetings that are chaired rather than directed, of recording and reviewing decisions, of giving and accepting responsibilities, all help to reinforce the rights and responsibilities that underpin democracy. In practice, however, the focus of civil society is often on changing the political system rather than on developing a body of participatory practice internally. Unless CSOs consciously do so they run the risk of reproducing, rather than changing, the norms and values of societies with authoritarian tendencies. The women's peace brigades in Northeast India are a good example of building the social basis for democracy from the ground upwards. This promotion of democratic ways of working should be encouraged, but not where it undermines the autonomy of the groups to decide upon their own priorities.

2. Realise that both meeting service needs and advocating for rights can be part of building the social basis for democracy

Whether organisations undertake advocacy or service provision, are 'traditional' or 'modern', big or small, donors should recognise that all can potentially contribute to a culture of democracy given that individual citizens have different identities and interests. The interests of CSO members may be immediate, such as access to a service, or strategic and concerned with longer term issues such as land tenure, access to the political system and policy makers, or changing gender roles. Civil society can thus play a crucial role in building experiences of democracy, but should do this through engaging in practical action that promotes inclusion as well as rights-based campaigning. The existence and activism of local associations which work to address people's basic needs often also strengthens arenas for negotiation and compromise. Donors should work with these existing associations and networks and their priorities, rather than artificially creating community groups or subverting their interests to outside development agendas.

3. Understand the political context, and realise that there are no short cuts to creating a culture of democracy from within

Take time to understand the political context and strengthen local manifestations of civil society on its own terms. In particular, remember that whilst external support can be positive if undertaken sensitively and with transparency, it can also lead to focus on external legitimacy rather than member interests. International links can lay civil society groups open to the charge of manipulation by external interests, and funding driven approaches may undermine civil society's potential to support political change in the long run by making them dependent upon funding which may be only available from government sources after the programme ends.

International actors must have a good understanding of the political context, and the interests and capacities of local civil society to avoid the pitfalls of being 'too political' or 'not political enough'. The Ethiopia and Kyrgyzstan cases demonstrate this fine line. On the other hand, in Kyrgyzstan, political civil society felt disgust at western hypocrisy as the gains of the Tulip Revolution evaporated and erstwhile international supporters avoided criticising the new government for geopolitical reasons. In Ethiopia, the state may be genuinely more concerned about unstable frontier regions than a rapid transition to multi-party democracy, and pushed back strongly against perceived pressure from the international community. Democratic norms and values underpinned by civil society are obviously still highly relevant. But interventions designed to strengthen civil society on its own terms, which are realistic in transitional contexts, are more likely to lead to a strong social basis for democracy in the long term.

There are several valid strategies for external actors wishing to support civil society efforts to build the social basis of democracy. Firstly, they should nurture CSOs with a strong constituency of the poor and marginalised by building their capacity to gather strength to influence policies in their favour. Secondly, they must strengthen links between sections of civil society, as shared purpose and strong networks are important to mobilise citizens and to engage with government. This 'thickening' of civil society and its relational capacities is central – as the social basis of democracy involves acknowledging the manifold diversity in all societies – and these linkages and relationships between diverse groups must come from within.

Summary of key points

Supporters of civil society should recognise that the social basis of democracy is often built by both service provision and advocacy in combination. Both political engagement and service work must be rooted in dedicated local constituencies, who are enhancing their civic participation by these activities.

Democratic and participatory ways of working within civil society and CSOs are essential, and effective in building democracy. The importance of this should not be underestimated.

Links and networks between civil society organisations are central to 'thickening' civil society and strengthening its relational capacities, and thus the social basis of democracy, as diverse interests gain recognition through processes of negotiation.

There is no short cut around the importance of local roots for civil society to be truly effective in influencing political change in the long term.

In support to civil society there is a need for a nuanced understanding of political context without being risk averse. Building the social basis of democracy through strengthening civil society is not the same as pushing a western liberal 'democratisation' agenda.

3

Promoting political accountability

Introduction

Elements of civil society are able to counterbalance dominant interests and power structures by monitoring the elites' conduct on various issues. Citizens, in principle, have the right to speak, but this is put into practice by activists in the myriad CSOs that remind political leaders that they hold decision-making power only in as far as they live up to their responsibilities to the people. By monitoring a wide range of particular interests, civil society groups exercise their right to engage in politics beyond a partisan party perspective – sometimes called politics with a 'small p'.[12] The general objective is to ensure that elites do not monopolise or abuse power through state, market or civic mechanisms but exercise it for the common good, through, at the very least, adherence to the rule of law.

The civil society function of holding those in authority to account for their political actions is an ancient one and has re-emerged recently as part of the 'good governance' agenda. With increasing privatisation and the reduction in the role of the state in many areas, calls for accountability have also spread from the state to the market – especially regarding market involvement in mainstream economic fields that have significant impact on populations such as extractive industries and the arms trade. We look at civil society's response to extractive industries in Chapter 4, and emphasise throughout the book that CSOs must also be accountable for their actions – primarily to their constituencies. This chapter focuses on civil society's function of promoting political accountability in relation to the state.

---

[12] In keeping with the sector's diversity, organisations within civil society will divide in their attitudes towards political accountability according to the interests of their particular constituency. Elite CSOs such as associations of municipalities or employers, chambers of commerce or informal groupings of military officers, are likely to be more supportive of authoritarian government that favours social stability at the expense of individual or collective rights. On the other hand, professional groups of lawyers may risk a great deal in insisting on the supremacy of the constitution and the rule of law over dictatorial governments – opposition to the military government's attempts in Pakistan to curb the Supreme Court being an eventually successful case in point.

> **Theoretical background**
>
> Alexis de Tocqueville's description of the vibrant associational life in 18th century America has been one of the most influential modern characterisations of civil society. Tocqueville described America as a society with an abundance of grassroots organisations, where people developed independent associations to argue and petition in promotion of their interests. The civic associations of America, he argued, provided a bulwark against majority rule by advancing marginal issues and the diverse causes of minority groups. Tocqueville contrasted this with European associations, which often purported to represent the will of the people but frequently resorted to violent means in the struggle for legitimacy and authority. In America, associations were notably *civil* in the promotion of their goals. He wrote; 'political associations in the United States are… peaceable in their intentions and strictly legal in the means which they employ; and they assert with perfect truth that they aim at success only by lawful expedients'.[xi] The strength of civil society in America was its vast number of grassroots associations that operated as social mechanisms to hold government accountable for policies that may only affect a minority of the population.
>
> In other contexts theorists have argued that the legitimacy of the state only comes from its acceptance by citizens. Without popular legitimacy, the state can only hold onto power by oppressive means. Therefore a successful state must be accountable to its citizens, earning its legitimacy by providing the services required by the populace and through mediating different demands from different groups. Alongside this, a vibrant civil society, such as that Tocqueville described, must be active in making these demands and holding the government to account.

The case studies in this chapter show how CSOs have held governments to account over abuses of power and position by the political elite. A range of formal and popular mechanisms and relationships provide channels to object to governments when they reject democratic processes and principles. One of the sharpest examples of promoting political accountability is that of human rights activists mobilising civil society against authoritarian regimes.

The first case study looks at the organised reaction of the families of the 'disappeared' across three continents. Many relatives of those who have disappeared tenaciously hold perpetrators to account by forming tight networks with strong popular appeal that only the most repressive regimes can ignore. The case shows that when CSOs are strongly embedded in loyal membership and there is effective South–South cooperation, strong steps can be made in promoting political accountability. Even though the work of such movements rarely results in the safe return home of the victim, it does send the message that the truth will be uncovered, even if it takes decades. The second case, from Kenya, demonstrates the important role of an independent and informed media sector in protecting individual citizens from violations by the authorities, in this case the police, in their treatment of individuals. However, those supporting civil society should note that this strategy requires considerable courage on the part of reporters, as they and their offices are particularly vulnerable to reprisal. It is also only effective in states with governments that regard themselves as at least somewhat accountable to all voices within civil society.

In The Gambia, the subject of the third case, the government was open to more progressive international law on child protection but this was not enough to bring about its enforcement in national legislation or the accompanying social change. Rather, it took civil society groups to hold the government accountable to the headline commitments it had made in international law. Civil society succeeded in reforming national law and positively influencing social practice through broad awareness raising combined with the mobilisation of various associations, including those of children themselves. This is a good example of North–South cooperation in which a civil society network of local and international actors makes the case for reform.

Civil society itself is not exempt from the duty to demonstrate legitimacy and accountability, abiding by the exacting standards set out in the values and objectives of the groups which make it up. As the fourth case in Bangladesh shows, civil society can fail this test when partisan and factional 'big P' politics co-opts it into its own patronage system. This co-optation by elites effectively eliminates civil society's capacity to provide an autonomous space for marginalised groups to express themselves, and interventions to redress this are necessary. The final case explores how INGOs' legitimacy comes into question when they compete for resources and space with southern civil societies. By doing so, they may undermine southern civil society's capacity for promoting political accountability. Accountability is not merely about a narrow governance advocacy approach, but about trying to facilitate a more level playing field for all civil society actors and more space for 'non-conformist' CSOs – not just well-connected, professional NGOs. The case testifies to the fact that it is hard for southern civil society actors to compete on their own ground with northern INGOs, and that ultimately, using local civil society as part of donors' aims to fulfil international norms and standards regarding accountability impoverishes the ability of local CSOs to defend citizens interests in the long term, even if it does ensure the continued availability of donor funding.

Case studies

3.1 Civil society and the rights of the 'disappeared'

Despite the steady spread of democracy, there are regimes across the world that have no qualms about eliminating civil society activists who seek to hold authoritarian elites to account. One of the cruellest forms of elimination is simply to make victims disappear. Each disappearance destroys the lives of numerous friends and relatives who may never know whether the disappeared individual is alive or dead. Repressive governments regard it a particularly effective tool against civil society as it spreads terror widely and paralyses opposition. Latin American regimes pioneered forced disappearance in the modern era during the wave of student and activist disappearances in the 1970s and 1980s, in particular Argentina's military junta of 1976–83. The technique has spread beyond the Americas among similarly violent regimes and at present Asia is the continent that reports the highest number of forced disappearances.

But alongside the spread of this ugly technique of repression has been a spread in civil society's demands for political accountability. Following the example set by Latin America, protest movements now exist wherever governments resort to this particular form of political repression. Relatives play a leading role in collective action. Argentinean mothers, for example, still parade in the Plaza Mayo outside government house in Buenos Aires every Thursday afternoon to ensure that the crimes perpetrated by the state against their children are never forgotten. Their vigilance is necessary to prevent Parliament from exonerating the armed forces through amnesty. Protest movements build on this committed membership to combine mutual support, campaigns for information and redress, and high level lobbying at the United Nations.

Regional federations

The world wide proliferation of enforced disappearance has compelled civil society to respond strategically to the threat. Civil society organisations responding to this issue are typically membership-based, underpinned by associations of relatives. With the foundation of FEDEFAM in Costa Rica in 1981, Latin America provided the model for organisational growth and regional federation:

'Initially, each relative begins an individual search. Later he or she meets relatives of other disappeared persons, and the tasks of searching and denouncing lead to the formation of associations of relatives. The growing awareness over time of the origins and aims of this form of repression, and the broadening role that the movement of the families of the disappeared played, brought us to cross national borders and establish communication with other Latin American countries. The collective analysis and understanding of the problem, and the obvious benefit of joining forces behind common objectives gave rise to FEDEFAM'.[xii]

Getting a similar federation up and running in Asia, however, was no easy task. There was, for instance, no common Asian language to facilitate communication and bind CSOs together. Although forced disappearance was common, organisations supporting relatives and victims were not. One of the first, Families of Victims of Involuntary Disappearance (FIND), was set up in 1985 to bring to light the more than 1,800 disappeared in the Philippines and to campaign for the ousting of President Marcos.

South–South cooperation

South–South cooperation between Latin American and Asian activists helped to build the new Asian federation. For example, FIND attended the 14th FEDEFAM Congress in Mexico in 1998, and a Jesuit priest who had set up an organisation to help relatives trace the disappeared during the vicious civil war in El Salvador between 1980-92 supported Asian organisations. South–South collaboration such as this bore fruit and by the end of the year the 'Asian Federation Against Involuntary Disappearances' (AFAD), was up and running. Along with FIND there were two other founder members; one from Sri Lanka and another from Jammu and Kashmir in India.

Cooperation between FEDEFAM and AFAD continued over the years in joint activities such as the Jakarta meeting of Asian and Latin American lawyers in 2000, and advice to AFAD in crucial housekeeping activities such as establishing a secretariat, developing statutes, strategies, work plans and commissioning evaluations of its work. By 2009, there were additional members in Indonesia, Nepal, Pakistan and Thailand, totalling nine in all.

As the movement spread, AFAD shared its experiences in 2003 with counterparts in West, East and South Africa and inspired the formation of the African Network Against Involuntary Disappearances (RADIF). Working together the three regional bodies of Africa, Latin America and Asia became a potent force in lobby and campaign efforts at the United Nations, particularly on the drafting of a Convention for protection against enforced disappearances.

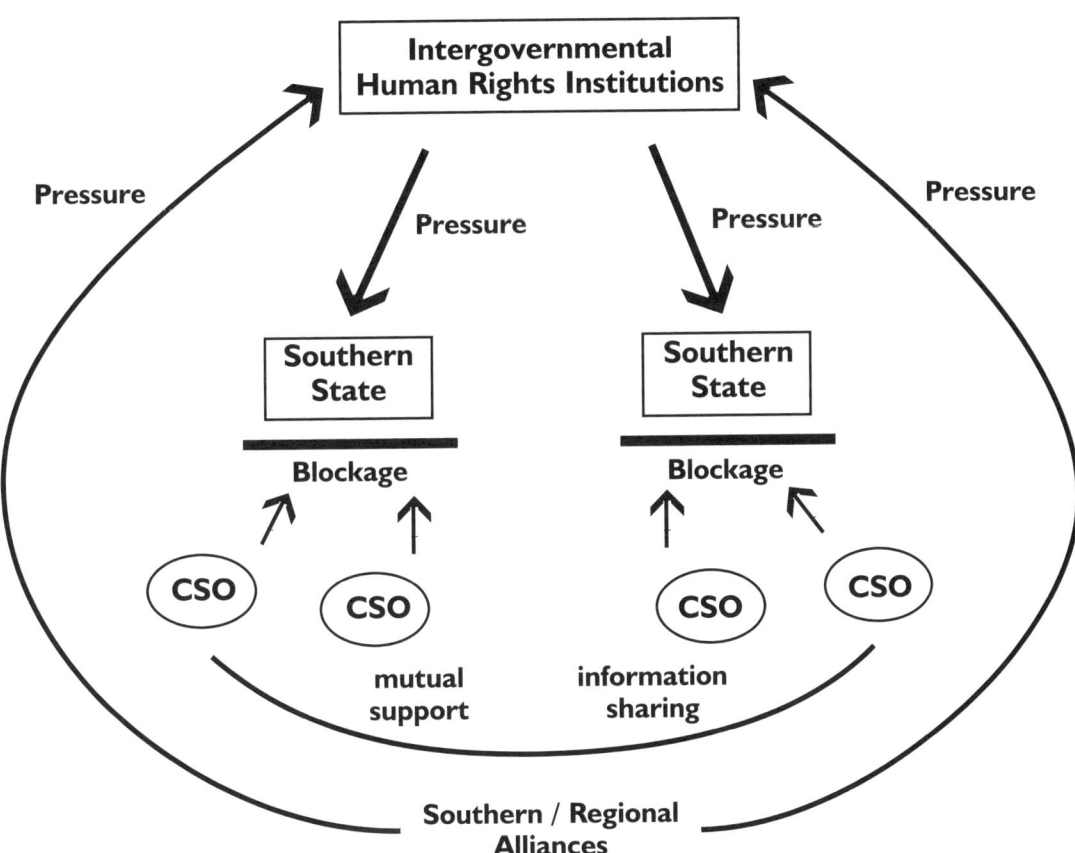

Adapted from Keck, M. and Sikkink, K. (1998) Activists beyond borders: advocacy networks in international politics, Cornell University Press.

Exposing enforced disappearance in Asia

Enforced disappearance in Asia is widespread but not well known owing to strict government control over information. The majority of the families of the disappeared in the region come from marginalised sectors of society, which rarely have the means to pursue their cases. In its day-to-day work AFAD publicises the issue and pressures Asian governments to respond to demands for accountability and to resolve past cases. At the regional level AFAD strengths the cooperation between member organisations, mobilises the attention of politicians and lawyers to the problem of disappearances, and contributes to campaigns against impunity.

Unlike their Latin American counterparts, who have made breakthroughs in achieving relatively concrete gains in achieving truth, justice and redress, the families of the disappeared in Asia have not yet succeeded in their demands for remedies. What makes their situation all the more difficult is the absence of regional human rights mechanisms which are necessary when local remedies are exhausted.

However, AFAD has brought about a unified Asian voice insisting that the 'disappearances' are extra-judicial killing, and Asia's governments can no longer claim that the disappeared are a problem only of Latin America. Approval in 2006 of the *United Nations Draft International Convention on the Protection of All Persons from Enforced or Involuntary Disappearances* signified a major breakthrough at international level and placed the plight of families of the disappeared in Asia and elsewhere on the UN agenda.

Continuing challenges

AFAD's greatest challenge came with the murder of its Chairperson, Munir Said Thalib, an Indonesian lawyer and the director of KontraS, a Jakarta-based NGO campaigning against disappearances. Munir was poisoned with arsenic on a flight in September 2004. The suspect, a pilot of the Indonesian national airline with alleged links to State Intelligence, was arrested and imprisoned, but later released. Harassment of KontraS continues to this day, as it campaigns for justice for Munir and other victims.

While the human rights movement in the Asian region has achieved successes, it is an ongoing struggle, and states continue to find new approaches to carrying out involuntary disappearances, for instance in the name of the 'war on terror'. AFAD believes it is imperative to strengthen the organisations of families of victims on the national, regional and international levels. It believes that stronger regional unity can contribute to the resolution of past cases and the prevention of future cases, but this needs to be linked to the struggle of civil society and grassroots organisations to ensure maximum impact.

Lessons

This case demonstrates the power of civil society in exposing covert criminal acts by governments against their citizens. Civil society's strength to do this is derived from broad-based solidarity, starting with a core membership of deeply affected members who are highly committed to redress and reform, supported by solidarity groups, churches and human rights lawyers. The crucial lesson that this case demonstrates is the importance and effectiveness of South–South cooperation in sharing legal, campaigning and organisational experience when working on difficult issues of political accountability. It shows that citizens who find the means of gathering together, linking across states and even continents, can bring about substantive change in the global human rights architecture and then begin to use it to claim reparations at the national level.

3.2 Engaging the media in human rights in Kenya

In democracies the media has multiple roles. Its market function is to make money for owners and investors, which it does by informing, entertaining and advertising. Its civic role is to hold government to account, ideally from an independent position but usually according to each owners' particular editorial stance. The freedom of the press, which supposedly underpins democracy, is therefore conditional even where state censorship does not exist. The challenge for civil society activists is to influence the media in ways which promote political accountability.

In Kenya, under the KANU party the state had a reputation for human rights violations, and used torture against its critics between 1963 and 1998. Most of these critics were arrested and detained without trial, while others were 'eliminated'. During the 1990s a civil society movement for change emerged which focused on human rights and good governance. CSOs sprung up to improve people's knowledge of rights and to articulate grievances against violent repression. From the outset, relations between the KANU government and civil society were tense. The government saw civil society and opposition political parties as one and the same thing. Civil society, on the other hand, saw KANU and the government as representing the status quo, not change for the better. After only five years of multi-party rule, the disputed election of December 2007 left trails of human rights violations and stifled democracy through a grand political coalition. In cooperation with human rights CSOs, the media took on an opposition role against a regime that had lost its legitimacy.

Human rights and advocacy journalism

One effective tool for promoting political accountability is 'advocacy journalism'. It engages the media to try to end state impunity for abusive human rights actions committed and to help hold perpetrators accountable. An advocacy organisation usually sends a team of human rights monitors to investigate allegations. If a case is reported and documented, consent is then obtained from the victim to use the documentation for publicity. Journalists then publish the case either in newspapers or the electronic media, and it can spark a national debate, and influence public opinion.

Kenya has a flourishing free press and human rights advocacy officers have a wide range of newspapers and radio stations to work with. Advocacy officers start by contacting different editors and journalists, discussing the concept of advocacy journalism, supplying information of the alleged violation case as well as specific questions for the journalists to take up. For the journalists, gathering information is often difficult, because of recent clamp downs on a free press, but still possible. After the journalist runs the story, the human rights organisation then decides how to intervene: making a case immediately or helping victims to launch a formal complaint to the independent Kenya National Commission on Human Rights.

Promoting justice for torture victims

The Independent Medico-Legal Unit (IMLU) and the consortium against torture apply advocacy journalism to defend the rights of torture victims. In cases of torture reported against the police, the victims often face obstacles in obtaining the necessary documentation to press charges. Victims complaining of torture or ill treatment by the police are required by law to report the allegations to the police station before being issued with police complaints form 'P3' which has to be certified by a police surgeon. Victims must prove that they were subjected to torture and that the act was intentional and systematic.

Advocacy journalism is a practical approach that, with determination, can make a real difference. Take the case of Kimani Njoroge, a 17-year-old street boy who was shot and arrested in Nairobi by the Kenya Police Reserve on allegations that he had committed a violent robbery. He was taken into custody and was repeatedly tortured. For five days, his friends and relatives looked for him and were often harassed and intimidated by police officers at the Central Police Station when they went there to seek assistance.

The case was reported to the IMLU, and there was an appeal through the media to track Kimani down. This eventually prompted the police to disclose his whereabouts. The media later published Kimani's ordeal in the newspapers, calling for the police to release him. The Nairobi Provincial Police Officer replied and acknowledged that Kimani was in police custody despite the central police earlier denying it.

IMLU responded by visiting the police station with journalists and doctors, and were denied access. Together they camped outside the police station and witnessed the police sneaking Kimani out and taking him to Kenyatta National Hospital. The activists followed the police convoy to the hospital and managed to get an interview with Kimani. He was blind, and doctors confirmed that Kimani had sustained a gunshot wound through his left eye. His health state and age did not deter the police from charging him for violent robbery.

Kimani remained in custody for eighteen months during his trial, and court reporters, using advocacy journalism, kept the case in the public eye. He was eventually acquitted because of lack of evidence. The outcome of the case prompted IMLU to make a complaint, but the police refused to issue the P3 form needed to make a formal complaint about torture. During the long battle, IMLU brought the case to the Commissioner of Police, the Attorney General and the Director of Criminal Investigations. While the resulting public debate about police violence was raging, the Commissioner of Police disbanded the Kenya Police Reserve and started an investigation into the Central Police Station. In this uphill struggle to hold authorities to account, Kimani now has his P3 form and has commenced the journey for justice.

Lessons

The media can be an effective channel for promoting political accountability. With determination, advocacy journalism can keep cases in the public eye where there is blatant injustice, like Kimani's, and exert pressure on the authorities. But this work can be dangerous for those involved, and depends on a free press. These tactics would have little chance of success in, for example, neighbouring Zimbabwe, and are under threat in Kenya as well.

3.3 The Gambia: making the rhetoric of children's rights real

Governments sign up to international human rights treaties for mixed motives. They often want their country to be seen as progressive and be carried away by the enthusiasm of the signing ceremony, but may be less committed to the reality of implementing the new rules. Civil society, by holding the government accountable to the commitments it has made, can help the executive arm of government apply the legislation, and build the support for it to be implemented throughout society.

In 1990, the Gambian government ratified the *UN Convention on the Rights of the Child*. However, for some, the concept of rights for children sounded like a western ploy to undermine African traditional culture. Compounding this, a lack of 'voice' in society, which affects many marginalised groups, left children few means to articulate wrongs committed against them and demand the right to effective protection. As a result harmful practices like female genital mutilation (FGM), sexual abuse, exploitation and violence carried on unhindered alongside the many positive aspects of children's lives in the country. Clearly the government's signing of a piece of international legislation alone was not going to make much of an impact on harmful practices.

In 2001 forty-eight organisations came together to form the Child Protection Alliance. To directly challenge the stigma associated with childhood abuse, the Child Protection Alliance decided to launch a thorough awareness-raising programme, rather than start with trying to confront the many loopholes in the law. This meant making NGO professionals more aware of the concept of child protection, carrying out research on specific forms of abuse and their prevalence, and communicating the results to opinion formers as well as members of the country at large, at the community level. To ensure that children themselves were engaged in the process, the Alliance sponsored a child-led advocacy group called 'Voice of the Young' to serve as a mouthpiece for children in The Gambia.

Over the best part of five years the Alliance made sure Voice of the Young were heard at every opportunity by radio, television and a constant stream of awareness-raising events. By the time the Alliance was ready to address the legal obstacles, these avenues for young people to speak had prepared public attitudes for change. Meanwhile the Alliance had completed its wide-ranging capacity building of front line workers, professionals and policy makers. Voice of the Young took advantage of an event attended by the President to appeal for a Children's Act. They were so persuasive that the President set Parliament to work and by June 2005, a Children's Act that was compliant with the UN Convention was voted into law.

Despite the fact that obstacles remain – for example, actually implementing the Act without sufficient budget or a dedicated Ministry for Children, and a lack of an outright ban on FGM – nonetheless issues that really matter to young people have begun to change. For example the law no longer criminalises children who fall victim to sexual exploitation, and the age of consent has been raised. State institutions such as schools can no longer use corporal punishment, and parents have started to report child abuse cases to the police and are even willing to stand as witnesses against perpetrators in court. Religious and community leaders regularly use Friday and Sunday sermons to encourage child protection. Issues of abuse and exploitation are even being discussed in the *bantaba*, the meeting place for village men. As a result attitudes are slowly changing.

Lessons
This case shows that legal reform from above is not enough to ensure real change. Civil society must get involved in promoting and demanding political accountability from governments to implement and facilitate measures for real change. International development practitioners hoping to support civil society to promote political accountability should note that addressing sensitive issues takes time and requires a strong capacity for mobilisation. Community involvement is needed alongside law and information. Legal reform is an important condition for policy change but alone it is not sufficient to guarantee children's rights, and likewise information alone is not enough to change deep-rooted traditional beliefs. People from various sections of society need to be actively involved – professionals, politicians, religious and community leaders, heads of families. Another key lesson is that helping children, or other marginalised groups that CSOs are working with, to access the media makes it possible for many more people to understand these groups' experiences and desires. The ongoing work in The Gambia also reminds us that legal and political reform must be accompanied by the creation of institutions that will enable its enforcement.

3.4 Listening directly to citizens in Bangladesh

Equal right of participation within civil society is relatively recent as a concept and is not universally acknowledged or observed. Elite capture of civic space is a constant reality that pervades democratic and undemocratic societies alike, and even CSOs with such missions may discriminate in practice despite their intentions to promote social justice and more equal societies. When civil society becomes co-opted by partisan and factional 'big P' politics, this severely reduces civil society's capacity to provide an autonomous space for marginalised groups to express themselves.

In the highly politicised society of Bangladesh, it is an open secret that most CSOs are tied firmly into the country's patronage system of 'big P' politics that govern every aspect of life, especially in the provision of services. Other forms of associational life, such as trade unions, social movements, and school boards are also firmly aligned in partisan and factional ways or with particular political parties.

As an alternative attempt to promote effective civil society demands for political accountability, one donor in Bangladesh has established a 'Reality Check' programme that exposes development professionals to the lives of the poor in a systematic and extended way. These links have the potential to open up civic space and 'small p' links between citizens and decision makers.

A lack of civic space

NGOs, once put forward as the solution to a factional civil society in Bangladesh, often have not lived up to being accountable 'downwards' to the marginalised. Many are urban based, limiting their meaningful contact with those living in rural poverty, with who they aim to work. At worst, they can merely function as intermediaries for patronage or dispensers of high interest, short-term loans. NGOs may have created admirable services but have not managed to help develop a strong local civil society able to engage with, and hence improve the accountability of, the state and government. Therefore as there is little independent civic space for voicing and acting upon shared concerns, it is not surprising that many citizens shun associational life. If at all possible they also avoid unpredictable public services and make their own arrangements with non-state providers of, for example, healthcare. In view of huge sums of aid money going directly to government, the absence of a genuinely autonomous civil society becomes a real problem for donors who are accustomed to mobilising local civil society as a watchdog. The aid industry is at a loss when there is no reliable means of monitoring the 'hands-off' funding mechanisms endorsed by the Paris Declaration, such as Sector Wide Approaches (SWAps).

The 'Reality Check' and policy influencing

There is a widening gap between government policy, supported by the aid industry, and lived experience, and a lack of channels for citizens to express their views about policies that directly affect them. To tackle this, the Swedish Embassy in 2007 commissioned a five year study aimed at 'listening to, trying to understand and convey poor people's reality'. Focused on health and education, the Reality Check study is undertaken in nine locations, urban, peri-urban and rural. It is combines listening approaches with more in-depth and less conventional methods, for example immersion, that is, staying in the homes of families living in poverty for several days and nights. This annual study report conveys the voices and opinions of people living in poverty to a wide range of policy makers involved in the two large-scale SWAp programmes. In addition to this immersion for the longitudinal research study, the Reality Check also encourages 'development partners' in the health and education sectors to undertake immersion programmes themselves and directly experience informal interaction with people living in poverty. Central government officials and development partners spend one night and two days with a family to 'help create ownership' of more responsive approaches. The main idea is that officials will develop respect and interest in people's voices and lives. Immersion has had some success in demonstrating to government officials the importance of listening. Many had never previously interacted with poor men and women whose lives they were supposed to improve.

Although this initiative did not emanate from Bangladeshi civil society, it is a notable attempt to open up civic space through promoting interaction between citizens in very different positions in society. The Reality Check study is accepted by government and the donors as an important citizen input and is expected to have policy influence and flag up issues for further review, for instance a finding of an unexpected preference for private health and education services over government ones even among the poor.

Lessons

Where civil society is weak and co-opted, those in power are out of touch with their target group, and so unable to make the voices of marginalised people heard higher up in government or development aid circles. This is important to try and redress in contexts such as Bangladesh, where civil society needs to be able to fulfil the function of promoting political accountability. This initiative importantly highlights the need to support ways of genuinely listening to citizen needs and opinions and creating direct relationships between those in power and the marginalised that will contribute to the opening up of civic space in the future.

3.5 Untangling the aid chain: northern NGO field presence in the South

By the late 1990s, through constant media exposure and insistent marketing, internationally operating NGOs from the North had won a position of dominance within 'aided civil society'. However, their adoption of the language of civil society, and apparent success masked a growing crisis of identity: were they really CSOs, or were they market operators, or simply contractors within the government-funded aid industry? Doubts began to arise on their real capacity to perform civic functions and their effect on local civil society's ability to hold government to account.

In April 2008, PSO, a membership association of fifty Dutch development agencies, organised a meeting, joined by Rajesh Tandon, the President of PRIA, a prominent Indian civil society organisation, to discuss the effects of northern NGOs moving South, a topical consequence of a shift in the aid industry towards decentralised funding. PSO's main focus is to strengthen civil society in the South by further developing the capacity of CSOs, and many of their members were establishing a field presence in the South. Given this, the obvious question for the group was; what does this increased northern presence mean for the capacity of southern civil society – does it strengthen it, is it neutral, or does it erode local capacity?

The last three decades have seen a massive increase of INGOs within southern and eastern civil societies. The embrace of these organisations by the aid system has made many of them bigger and stronger in terms of profile, capacities and resources. However, it has not necessarily made the civil societies in locations where they work more robust and sustainable. One of the reasons for this is that northern INGOs often treat southern CSOs as a means to achieve northern-led development goals. This can erode local organisations' capacity to set their own goals, build a strong local base and play a meaningful role in working for the poor and marginalised.

Many PSO members claimed that their direct presence made capacity building faster, smoother and easier and so was beneficial to the southern CSOs. By responding to donor tenders in consortia with local CSOs, the northern agencies aimed to build local CSOs' capacities 'on the job'. On the negative side the presence of northern agencies was found to introduce unfair competition for staff and resources as well as taking over the role of the local CSOs. The effect is to reduce the role of southern civil society in its own field. It also hampers the space of local CSOs to organise, grow and push for social change, as their northern agency partners are not useful for sensitive advocacy. When INGOs lead on advocating, the issues they raise about politics can easily be discredited by opponents as a foreign intervention.

The decentralisation of northern INGOs to the South can limit the space available for southern CSOs to promote political accountability by advocating as independent actors. Donors present their decentralisation of funds in the light of the Paris Declaration's uneasy combination of lofty ideals (local ownership) and administrative efficiency (results-based management). However, although competitive in-country bidding for funds is encouraged, local organisations often notice that signing up as a junior partner of a European development agency is the only way to access these funds. Northern INGOs conducting advocacy on behalf of southern civil society have even more ambivalent effects, as the case on Ethiopia in Chapter 2 highlighted.

Thus, the meeting highlighted that northern INGOs deciding on a field presence in the South face a dilemma between their institutional and developmental aims. The need for resources to survive and continue their work compels them to follow decentralised donor funding to the field, and set their agendas around the latest international norms and standards. However by doing so, the agencies come into conflict with their developmental aim to strengthen local civil society, helping to build strong local CSOs which will work for the interests of the poorest and most marginalised, and implicitly, to work themselves out of a job. This conflict is especially pronounced in regard to this function of civil society's capacity to promote political accountability.

Lessons

With field offices in the South, northern INGOs are facing a series of contradictions that they need to confront in the interests of accountability. Some argue that they are an integral part of local civil society because many of their staff and now their resources are derived in-country;[13] and others claim that they form part of a borderless global civil society. However, good donorship entails consciously taking into consideration the effect that northern agencies make on civil society in the South. Those that already have a presence in the South should try to limit their domination of civic space, and try to create space for local CSOs ability to demand political accountability, by:

- Not entering into competition for funds with local organisations.
- Transferring as many decision making powers as possible to local partners.
- Supporting local organisations, strengthening their capacities and move them to the forefront, even when it is about accessing local EU and other funds.
- Limiting numerical presence to limit power imbalances.
- Keeping similar wage levels to avoid brain-drain.

---

[13] Some INGOs have now started to argue that their localisation has created local CSOs, but this can be questioned by referring the governance structure of the local office – is it locally or internationally based? Where are agendas set in reality? And would the office be sustainable with less foreign funding?

Recommendations

The cases here have highlighted that promoting political accountability is much more than just support for advocacy on governance issues. Instead, a wide range of civil society actors must call for, work towards, and monitor their particular interests. Civil society's engagement in 'small p' politics tries to ensure that elites do not monopolise or abuse power but exercise it for the common good. These demands on the state must come from within. Organisations from other countries' civil societies should respect local agency but be willing to show solidarity and respond to invitations for support.

1. Invest in South–South cooperation for political accountability at an international level
CSOs with loyal and dedicated membership bases can make an impact beyond their size, and even more so when they link with other similar organisations. An effective way to help them promote political accountability is to support South–South cooperation in the form of regional alliances and global networks. These organisations can learn from other actors operating in similar contexts, and lobby at different levels. They can make an impact on the global level using the universal language of human rights, and at lobbying at the regional level can lead to regional systems for protection of human rights which may be more effective than universal bodies.[xiii] A good model of this was explored in the first case of the chapter. As the 'disappearance' model of state-sponsored terror spread from Latin America to Asia and Africa, it was also followed by the solidarity, know-how and resources needed to confront it. The organisations in different countries formed regional alliances and global networks around the language of human rights, and thus have made an impact on the global level, that will hopefully increase pressure for change in their national contexts.

2. Recognise the value of 'human rights' as catalyst
International human rights instruments can be a powerful catalyst for civil society work to promote political accountability. The successes and challenges of civil society's ability to promote political accountability in our case studies must be placed in the context of the global expansion of human rights architecture, which since the Second World War has had a dramatic influence on civil society. Although systems are more strongly developed in some continents than others, civil society activism has made a momentous shift from needs-based to rights-based approaches.

However, those supporting work within the framework of international human rights must bear in mind that the ultimate objective of these instruments is to create change within national contexts at the grassroots, and agendas for change must follow local priorities. Given the high international profile of rights – and the aid conditionalities attached to them – governments may give theoretical support to human rights. Civil society participation and mobilisation around these headline commitments must be encouraged, as the case from The Gambia demonstrated. A commitment to a treaty on children's rights catalysed civil society to work to raise awareness and mobilise for change in practice, and to call for government to show accountability to their commitments by building them into national law. The legal framework is important for building accountability on the basis of human rights. Human rights campaigners need access to courts at the national levels as well as the regional and international, and in some contexts civil society's capacity to investigate and report on the internal human rights situation may be stifled, as in Ethiopia, Russia, Singapore and Zimbabwe where new civil society laws prohibit the defence of human rights.

3. Use media engagement

The combination of a human rights perspective with an independent and informed media sector can lead to determined and effective calls for accountability from authorities. However, supporters of this type of work must remember that this can carry high risks for their partners. A prerequisite to using the media as an effective counterbalance to ineffective or corrupt political accountability is that the media is independent and that citizens can contribute to it. More broadly, the media has been important in allowing CSOs to uncover or publicise local issues, for example famine in India, which can otherwise remain hidden to policy makers and the wider public. The media can also provide the oxygen of publicity for campaigns designed to hold the authorities to account for local abuses of power. ICT has a role to play, especially for organising mass protests where repressive regimes, like Iran's, deny the right to peaceful demonstration. On highly-charged occasions like this it can effectively work around the state-controlled media, at least in the short term.

4. Open up civic space for the marginalised

The lived experience of common citizens all too rarely reaches the world of NGOs and government. Practitioners who have lost touch with the ordinary people the aid system is intended to help, should carry out their own 'reality check', and spend time engaging with the marginalised, as well as promoting this sort of encounter between marginalised citizens and central government officials. INGOs in particular need to be more self-aware about their institutional constraints, which hinder them from operating in the interests of the poor and marginalised. They should respect and explicitly create space for 'non-conformist' actors, whether they are social movements or membership based organisations that aim at improving local conditions, or those taking an explicitly political approach. Many are expressions of ancestral culture and tradition that aim at improving local conditions, rather than taking an explicitly political approach, but the importance of 'space' for these actors as a part of a society which is politically accountable to all voices is often ignored. Other non-conformist CSOs have evolved into large membership associations with very specific demands on the state. Examples include movements of slum dwellers, landless peoples, or homeless people; for example Dalits in India and indigenous peoples in Latin America. These and others do not accept a status quo that relegates entire population groups as second class citizens. The strength of these groups is that they are creating their own civic spaces to demand needs and rights, rather than being 'invited' into solutions managed by NGOs. Alternative budgeting is another good example of opening up civic space in new ways. It has a track record in promoting local accountability with a high degree of civic participation in India and Africa and especially in Brazil. The idea is to ensure that pro-poor municipal budgets are developed, approved and implemented in a participatory manner that makes best use of the potential voting power of the marginalised.

5. Building local capacity for advocacy is essential

Developing the local capacity for advocacy is essential if development practitioners are to avoid the pitfalls involved in undertaking their own heavy-handed advocacy whose agenda is clearly not based in a constituency. Promoting political accountability through advocacy is unlikely to be successful when local civil society is supplanted or brought into an unequal relationship with northern actors. Donors are generally on solid ground when supporting local civil society to promote 'small p' political accountability as in The Gambia child protection case; supplanting local civil society in 'big P' action, as in the earlier Ethiopia case, can backfire badly. Patiently supporting local groups to find their voice and to connect with others is of much more enduring benefit.

Summary of key points

Civil society's strength to call for political accountability is ultimately derived from broad-based solidarity, starting with a core membership of deeply affected members who are highly committed to redress and reform.

South–South and regional cooperation in sharing legal, campaigning and organisational experience is important and effective in enabling civil society to promote political accountability.

When a government has a headline commitment to international human rights, civil society can use this as a catalyst to organise and press for change.

Legal reform from above is not enough to ensure real change, civil society must get involved in promoting and demanding political accountability from governments to implement and facilitate measures for real change.

The media and 'advocacy journalism' can be an effective tool for CSOs to uncover or publicise local issues, and thus promote political accountability for transparency and rights. But it is also important to remember that communities need to influence and work with the media. ICT has a role to play in empowering local communities to work around state-controlled media and injustice.

Where civil society is weak, CSOs may be partisan, elite and out of touch with marginalised people, and it will be difficult for civil society to fulfil the function of promoting political accountability. Creating relationships between citizens in different positions has potential for opening up civic space and enhancing political accountability.

Northern INGO field presence in the South brings up a series of uncomfortable contradictions about accountability. Demands for 'accountability' to donors may weaken local organisations' capacity for accountability and legitimacy in relation to constituents, and thus their ability to promote political accountability more broadly. Northern INGOs must enable 'non-conformist' CSOs to promote political accountability through their autonomous agendas and approaches.

4

Producing trust, reciprocity and networks

Introduction

Gathering together in 'civic communities' – horizontal organisations such as cultural clubs, local associations and religious communities – is important not only for organising but also builds relationships between people. In bringing individuals together to interact, 'social capital' is created. Social capital is about reinforcing trust and creating the environment for all sorts of transactions to take place in the assumption that they will be honoured. Trust, reciprocity and networks are used to solve common problems, and the range of associations between individuals from different institutions is also crucial to the working of any market. It is also essential to remember that each individual and household play many roles at once within civil society, and create trust in many different directions. An individual might be a member of the local parent-run play group, a trade union, a neighbourhood association, and a football club. In international development many agencies try to place people into just one category, for example; the village development committee or the women's club, rather than recognising that it is the diversity of multiple relationships which strengthens civil society.[14]

---

[14] In See Appendix 3, which documents the diversity of informal associations in rural areas of Ethiopia, whose memberships often overlap.

> **Theoretical background**
>
> Tocqueville's observations about associational life in America (see theoretical background in Chapter 3) have more recently been developed and expanded by Robert Putnam in his more narrow concept of 'civic community'. Civic community constitutes one element of civil society; horizontally-structured organisations 'that are more or less mutual, cooperative, symmetrical, and trusting'.[xiv] Such organisations, which include everything from extended families and bowling clubs to religious communities and interest groups, generate 'social capital'. Social capital consists of trust, reciprocity and networks that enable people to more easily solve collective action problems. Voluntary cooperation, Putnam argues, is easier in a community that has inherited a substantial 'stock' of social capital because people have confidence that others will not defect out of self-interested opportunism. Several caveats are often added to the argument that civil society produces social capital: not all civil society organisations generate the same amounts of social capital, for instance, think tanks produce less than neighbourhood watch schemes, and social capital may be used for 'darker' purposes; for instance, criminal rings.[xv]

Civil society has a crucial role in building trust, reciprocity and networks in situations where they have been absent. Strong membership bases for civil society organisations and social movements mean that they have the trust and solidarity needed to tackle large scale, persistent inequality. Social movements are membership groups that take rights-based collective action for their members' needs[xvi] and often channel social capital particularly strongly, first and foremost in listening to their members.[15] The first case in this chapter explores the social movement of the homeless and poorly housed in Brazil, where the movement has both confronted and engaged with public authorities. Membership-based social movements have a strength of capacity that is derived from the energy of their members, and from listening to them rather than 'professionalising' for the aid industry. This case also illustrates the strength of social movements in crossing the advocacy–service delivery divide. They are primarily about improving the conditions of a particular group – the homeless, in the case of Brazil – yet their claims are also most likely to be framed in the language of rights.

A second case from Costa Rica shows how new technologies can facilitate the building of equitable and democratic networking interactions between CSOs which greatly increase both their collective impact and individual capacities. When the US extended its free trade agreement to Central America, the government in Costa Rica called a referendum. There was little doubt that the 'YES' vote would win because the government invested heavily in media campaigning to promote the agreement. In the absence of resources, civil society fell back on voluntary mobilisation and ICT expertise to take its message out to associations across

---

[15] According to Earle (2004) the definition of social movement is difficult to pin down and subject to debate, as the term is widely used to refer to diverse phenomena. Earle's definition of southern social movements focuses on an essence of 'rights-based resistance', often in demand of basic rights for members, or against damaging government initiatives. She sees campaigning networks and NGOs as one step removed from the core definition.

the country. The 'NO' vote came close to winning, delivering a clear message to government that civil society's social capital was strong, and could be converted into political capital.

Without trust at the local level in civil society, between authorities and those on the margins, little can be done to bring about substantial or sustainable change. Building trust is a long-haul investment, but when it comes together makes the rhetoric of participation real. The third case, from Suriname, is a good example of an initiative which made power difference transparent at the level of the local community, and consequently created space for negotiation around development initiatives from which everyone gains – for example rubbish collection. Nigeria, the site of the fourth case, is a country sorely lacking trust, where long periods of military rule have meant that the relationship between state and civil society was conflictual, with the state essentially a law unto itself. However, Nigerian CSOs are developing skills and confidence to engage with, and demand reciprocity from, both the government and multinationals – at the most sophisticated level through their shareholders, using the investment clout of European churches as leverage.

Civil society's ability to produce trust, reciprocity and networking is an essential function of more just, egalitarian societies. This is because stronger and more diverse linkages and relationships within and between different groups, have the potential to address power relationships that cause poverty and marginalisation. The final case, from Tajikistan, is a warning against a romanticised view of 'local community', where social capital may exist within but not between groups. Unless there is a meeting place between the minority elite and the ruled, power and ownership will always concentrate at the top of the pyramid. Carefully designed interventions with in-depth contextual understanding are necessary to avoid this. Donors should not be risk averse, getting stuck in fulfilling aid industry targets, but must realise that beyond these targets is a need to encourage the building of social capital and to tackle local power dynamics.

Case studies

4.1 Sao Paulo's homeless citizens' movement

We know that tackling poverty and inequality is not a simple task. A crucial element that is often missing from NGO work is a strong membership base and sense of solidarity. This case shows how a housing social movement in Brazil contains the trust and social capital needed to take effective action.[16]

With a population over 190 million, Brazil is Latin America's largest country. Its economy is also the healthiest in the region and it has recently positioned itself well amongst world decision-makers on trade issues. However, behind the progressive image, where the popular President has a trade union background, lies extreme inequality. The richest 10% of Brazilians receive 50% of the nation's income, while the poorest 10% receive less than 1%. Deprived of land, housing, employment, health care and education, Brazil's multi-million

---

[16] This case is based on ESRC-funded research carried out by Lucy Earle.

strong army of the poor is increasingly mobilised to claim a stake in the country's new wealth. To get a better understanding of their dynamics, an INTRAC researcher spent 2008 in Sao Paulo with organisations linked to the *Movimento sem Teto*, a citizens' movement for low income housing – literally for the 'roofless'.

Root causes of homelessness

Sao Paulo's housing problem is self-inflicted. Instead of integrating all social groups as the mega-city expanded to its present population of 20 million, the authorities simply pushed the poor to the periphery in a long sequence of often violent evictions. The result is the infamous *favela* areas of unregistered settlements ruled by shanty town gangsters. Not surprisingly living in the *favela* carries stigma amongst better-off citizens. Services are very poor and for anyone lucky enough to have work it can take two hours to reach the city.

Constitution and occupation

However the homeless are not without recourse. The *Movimento* is large, visible and well organised – and the law is on its side. Under the 1988 constitution, citizenship confers the right to housing, education and health care. By neglecting to provide adequate housing within the city proper, the authorities are automatically in the wrong. No one contests this; decent housing is perceived as a condition of full citizenship by city residents, policy makers and academics as well as the *Movimento*. All recognise that having a house and an address in the 'legal city' is essential to claim other rights, for example, to education and health, which make up the fundamentals of social citizenship.

The *Movimento* cultivates allies and networks amongst NGOs specialised in legal aid, and with figures of authorities such as the city ombudsman and the public prosecutor, in order to take the state to court. It has had successes, for example against the municipal government in restoring housing benefits to families evicted from properties declared unsafe. As a result many movement members are now training as lawyers so they can take on these cases themselves.

None of this engagement with the courts prevents the *Movimento* from staging illegal acts of its own, usually in high profile occupations of empty government property. These hazardous operations bring them into direct conflict with the police but they also generate favourable publicity and energise the membership. Again, the law can arguably be on the side of the *Sem Teto*, as property left empty contravenes the national constitutional requirement for urban infrastructure to fulfil some 'social function'.

NGOs' role

The conditions faced by the *Sem Teto* forces them to fight 'on all fronts' regardless of legality. At the same time the *Movimento* openly support politicians who favour their cause. Whilst solidarity and trust are built between members of the movement, and networks with authorities formed, NGOs are reluctant to engage, for fear of illegality and involvement in 'big P' politics. Even so there are useful tasks that NGOs can undertake in support of the movement, for example in helping train members as lawyers. There are also good reasons for the *Movimento* not to engage with externally funded projects, as their deadlines have been known to push the *Movimento* into inappropriate action to please the donor.

Lessons
This case testifies to the importance of social capital between the oppressed, where a strong membership base is effective to mobilise for change. Large-scale solidarity movements like these can best grow institutionally and yet retain their independence when they raise their resources mainly through their membership, like trade unions – rather than through the aid industry. The powerful use of constitutional law by the movement suggests that wherever possible local civil societies should focus lobbying efforts on changes in their own country's legal systems. If authorities are, at least to a basic level, democratic and receptive, social movements can benefit more immediately and effectively from rights enshrined in national law, where the duty bearer is close at hand, than the distant international structure of human rights.

These lessons point to the potential for NGOs to help by supporting the capacity of social movements to engage with their national policy and legal contexts. Relationships between NGOs and social movements may challenge NGOs' established ways of working but can also provide a way to tackle many INGOs lack of membership bases in recipient countries, which undermines the legitimacy of claims that they are 'bridges of people', facilitating partnerships between citizens of different countries.

4.2 A virtual social movement in Costa Rica

New technology provides a cheap and effective method of networking and campaigning for CSOs worldwide. In this case, in Costa Rica, CSOs with diverse remits came together for one campaign primarily organised and promoted through a shared online platform. The trust built via equal and participatory collaboration on the campaign greatly increased both CSOs' collective impact and individual capacities. The networks and accompanying social capital and trust built between those working in Costa Rican civil society have a lasting impact far beyond the particular campaign, providing a clear message to government that civil society's social capital is strong, and can be converted easily into political capital.

The 'Patriotic Movement "NO"' was an ICT-based protest in Costa Rica against the spread of the US Free Trade Agreement to Central America. Five Central American countries were to hold a referendum on the agreement, but in Costa Rica the result seemed a foregone conclusion; government funding made sure that over 90% of publicity in the mainstream media urged a 'YES' vote. The movement in favour of 'NO' consisted of a broad range of CSOs of every level and sector. They represented the country's most important social movements – of students, women, trade unions, farmers, academics, advocates of gay rights and environmentalists.

They could not compete with the YES vote funding so instead they mobilised their collective expertise in ICT, especially via the internet and radio. There was no question of hiring a flash PR company, so they made a virtue of diverse voices and democratic credentials. No organisation took the lead and there was no single champion, rather the vision was to link that diversity and share the work according to the capacity and creativity of each organisation. For example, those familiar with policy discourse 'translated' the dense CA-FTA documentation into a more accessible language, while others transformed this information into web-friendly materials and uploaded it onto various online platforms. Since many in the country had no access to the internet, others downloaded the materials and produced CDs, brochures, flyers, stickers, and t-shirts, to support community based campaigning.

Community based information initiatives sprung up around the country, as 'Patriotic Committees'. The information gave rise to a wealth of initiatives such as discussion groups, forums, calls for demonstrations, petitions and email appeals to public figures. The organisations disseminated the messages from the campaigning through blogs, social networking tools, videos, podcasts and so on. Two spaces with particular added value for the movement were YouTube and the platform 'Con Costa Rica'.[17] The combination of these came into its own during the referendum campaign itself, hosting about 1,500 videos on the topic. The interactive nature of the Con Costa Rica website, which even launched the country's first online funding campaign, showed new technology's potential as an innovative social mobilisation strategy.

In the end, the Patriotic Movement 'NO' lost the referendum, but only by a very small margin. The networks and social organisation generated along the way represent a victory for the social movement, as do the higher levels of political commitment and capacity of civil society to analyse and mobilise around complex issues.

Lessons

The movement folded soon after the referendum, though it would be a mistake to regard this as a weakness. Rather, the multiple relationships and associations built through the campaign will enable a greater level of social capital between those working for political change in Costa Rica. New technology can facilitate networks that last far beyond specific campaigns. The government was also forced to pay attention to the fact that civil society expected a high level of transparency and accountability and could mobilise peacefully, but vigorously, to insist on it.

4.3 Making voices count in Suriname

The first two cases have looked at the value of social capital in civil society where it is taking more of an oppositional engagement to the state. This case demonstrates the value of developing links between citizens and authorities at the local level, where more active citizens, more links between citizens, and greater trust between civic organisations and authorities can make a big difference.

The case looks at how producing trust between the marginalised and the authorities at the local level is essential to enable the interactions that create change for the better. Projekta is a Dutch organisation working for women in development. It spent six years strug-

---

[17] See www.concostarica.com

gling unsuccessfully to build and link social capital in the mainly rural and agrarian Nickerie district of western Suriname, before managing to establish participatory structures and processes between local civil society and the authorities.

In 2001, the organisation started with capacity building for community organisations but over time it became clear that training and mentoring were not enough to bring about change in the entrenched and highly centralised power structure. Such was official distrust of non-government action that none of the initiatives put forward by the CSOs were ever accepted – not even a voluntary rubbish collection scheme. Patronage and 'big P' clientelism ruled all relationships in Nickerie, where those in charge interpreted any suggestion for improvement as unwelcome criticism. Displeased patrons could lead to even fewer opportunities for the have-nots. So the few independent CSOs got discouraged and faded away.

Another opportunity for greater civil society action came with a government decentralisation programme, which selected Nickerie as a pilot. Participation was supposedly an integral part of the programme, but this also proved a disappointment as 'participation' meant desultory hearings followed by provision of free labour for minor infrastructure works. Clearly nothing would change without an acceptable process for participation by ordinary citizens in decision-making.

Not to be put off, Projekta came up with the idea of a policy monitoring system in which participation was to be taken seriously – as a *right* – and the goal was democratised governance. This time there was a clear rights-based methodology based upon on shared planning, implementing and monitoring of activities from an agreed, community-led needs assessment. The process included everyone – Members of Parliament, CSOs, Ministry and service sector representatives, the business community and individual citizens. This time, something changed. At the first meeting, the gathering decided on official rubbish dumps, speed bumps outside schools, a maintenance rota for the sports stadium and a new public transport link for an isolated hamlet. By the second meeting, six months later, the group reviewed the achievements and set themselves new targets.

What provided the trust necessary to finally undertake effective community work? The secrets to success, in Projekta's opinion, were complete transparency, inclusiveness, and taking the time at the start of the project to build a shared understanding of working towards tasks perceived as 'win-win'. With a rights-based approach and a community-led needs assessment, social and power relations were transparent for all to see. The inclusion of a diverse range of organisations in participatory processes helped citizens become less fearful and apathetic, and the officials see the benefits of strengthening their popularity through being more willing and responsive to working for the community.

Lessons

Across all different governance conditions there is a need to build social capital between the powerful and marginalised at the community level. Sustainable results need substantial and strategic participation. But it takes false starts and patience to bring about change in the way decisions are made, and by whom. Above all it takes time to build trust between a diversity of local actors. NGOs need to acknowledge that their work does not support civil society merely by default, as a natural by-product of their usual business. To strengthen civil society through building trust, NGOs should challenge the status quo in local power dynamics. They can do this by helping to create associations with supporting processes and structures, even if it is painstaking, rather than 'just doing' the local work that needs to be done. Whilst in this case an international NGO provided the stimulus for networking between previously isolated stakeholders, it took years to achieve a breakthrough – arguably showing that in order to support civil society sustainably INGOs need great commitment to slowly building participation over time.

4.4 Can Nigeria take on extractive industries?

Many countries are faced with the sore need to build trust where it is utterly lacking. This case looks at how people and organisations across civil society in Nigeria are gradually engaging with one another and with the authorities to demand greater transparency from government and multinationals.

Military dictators have ruled Nigeria for 28 of the last 42 years, enriching themselves and their supporters from the country's vast oil wealth. The relationship between the state and civil society reached its lowest ebb when Ken Saro-Wiwa, founder of MOSOP – Movement for the Survival of the Ogoni People, was executed in 1995.

The Ogoni are one of the ethnic groups living in the Niger Delta, which had become an environmental disaster zone thanks to extensive spillages of crude oil resulting , from poorly regulated oil extraction. This oil-rich region covers nine out of Nigeria's 36 states and is home to 27 million of the estimated total 155 million Nigerians. The Delta is the cash cow of the Nigerian state, providing more than 80% of revenue, paying for a new-age capital in Abuja and an elite bureaucracy, rewarding the politically well-placed with fabulous sums. MOSOP risked upsetting the international oil companies who kept the oil flowing, and by extension the centres of Nigerian power and privilege. Like most Nigerians, the Ogoni live in acute poverty, see little positive development in their state, and want to benefit materially from the vast wealth of the oil industry. Some use the term 'resource curse' as a shorthand for the conditions in places like Nigeria, where the exploitation of a country's natural resources to benefit the few rather than the many causes widespread corruption, rising inequality, social unrest and environmental degradation.

International outrage at Ken Saro-Wiwa's execution prompted the Commonwealth to expel Nigeria for three and a half years. Even the transition to democracy in 1998 could not heal the relationship between civil society and authorities. But two examples show civil society making efforts to gradually build mechanisms for greater reciprocity and trust, as they promote transparency in the extractive industry.

The Church and campaigns for Corporate Social Responsibility
Shell has been in the Niger Delta since its first commercially important oil strike over 50 years ago. But for the people of the Niger Delta, oil has meant wrenching poverty brought about by wholesale violation of their rights: civil and political, economic, social and environmental. How was it that Shell, winner of environmental awards in Europe, could knowingly be

poisoning villagers and condemning them to a slow toxic death in their callous rush for oil?[xvii] Multinational oil companies have also been complicit in violations of the rights to life and fair trial. Catholic missionaries from Ireland had long witnessed the impact of Shell's Nigeria operations on the health and livelihoods of farming and fishing communities, and the Church started to mobilise after the execution of Ken Saro-Wiwa in 1995.

The Church's campaign for greater Corporate Social Responsibility was a joint operation by two organisations, one in Europe and the other in Port Harcourt, the capital of Rivers State. In the UK, The Ecumenical Council for Corporate Responsibility (ECCR) was established in 1989 to raise awareness of congregations in Ireland and the UK about responsible investment. This involved demanding accountability of UK companies working in distant parts – often with capital generated from Church investments.

In Nigeria, growing out of a citizens' movement already active in the struggle for corporate justice and responsibility, the Centre for Social and Corporate Responsibility (CSCR) was established in 2001 as 'the eyes and ears' of multinational company shareholder groups in the Niger Delta. It provided a steady stream of evidence, collection of which was facilitated by the credibility it enjoyed as the partner of European faith-based shareholders. This gave CSCR access, for example, to the highest levels of Shell management in Nigeria.

For its part ECCR had pioneered a method of engaging with the board of Shell as shareholders in the company, successfully putting forward resolutions for discussion at annual general meetings. Over the years it realised that Shell's management was adept at dragging its feet over real change on the ground and so in 2007 it went straight to Shell's governing board and arranged a meeting with the Social Responsibility Committee, which was chaired by Wim Kok, former Prime Minister of The Netherlands. CSCR was present to hear just why Shell management had failed to put in place its own new standards of operation and community engagement in the Delta region.

Faith shareholder networks can be effectively connected both with communities worldwide that suffer the impacts of corporate abuses, and the centres of power where the headquarters of extractive multinationals are based. The solidarity based approach here used trust connections to develop a model of evidence-gathering and dissemination with shareholder networks to get corporates to wake up to their social obligations.

Accountability mechanisms for extractive industries

The government of Nigeria has also shown signs of wanting to move on, not least due to problems in the Delta region with 'uncivil society', social movements that take up arms. As an effort to rebuild trust with the electorate, late in 2003 Nigeria joined EITI, an accountability mechanism which asks international companies to publish what they pay for mineral, oil or gas rights and host governments to do the same for what they earn.

The initiative arose from a campaign called 'Publish What You Pay'. The idea is that independent validation of the figures can discourage the abuses that fuel the 'resource curse' in so many countries and release funds for essential development tasks. It was the initiative of a group of mainly European international NGOs but EITI has since spread to 70 countries, with the support of half a dozen OECD country donors. Some of the worlds' biggest oil and gas companies also signed up alongside their government partners.

By February 2004 the Nigerian EITI (NEITI) had set up its accountability mechanism – a multi-stakeholder group with the membership of relevant government departments, extractive industry companies, and CSOs. Its steering group became the first platform where civil society and government came together to discuss policy matters. The group carried out a series of 'road shows' beyond the capital so that government and industry could present their cases and listen to feedback from civil society.

The system was then formalised in an Memorandum of Understanding between government and civil society. A Secretariat soon followed, with quarterly meetings with a liaison officer appointed by CSOs. It produced an audit of the extractive industry in Nigeria covering 1999-2004. It also undertook work to strengthen capacities for advocacy within civil society by undertaking a training of trainers programme for 150 CSOs across the country. By 2007 a NEITI Bill passed into law and the National Assembly appointed a liaison officer of its own to deal with inquiries by CSOs.

Lessons

Building trust is slow when it has been dramatically undermined. Strong divisions between the marginalised and national elites do not lend themselves to recipes for immediate change. Governments need to face up to their responsibility for the local effects of resource extraction, and accompanying economic policies. Accountability mechanisms such as the ones in these cases are a necessary basis for the process of restoring relationships of trust and reciprocity between state and citizens, and throughout society. The conditions for success are that on the one hand governments overcome their hostility to citizens' organisations and engage directly with them in good faith; and on the other hand civil society takes an active and constructive part in policy discussions and decision making.

Civil society initiatives such as the Church campaign may contain within them the trust for a productive partnership for campaigning that is strong both in terms of an evidence base and access to multinationals. In a globalised world social movements can combat oppression at home by deploying links with northern civil society in support of their home-grown social capital. However, the process of changing corporate policy is often easier than bringing about change on the ground. Shell's failure to improve its social responsibility in practice bodes ill for regions exploited by less familiar companies, especially when they come from countries which do not necessarily subscribe to high standards of corporate responsibility.

4.5. Pervasive power dynamics in Tajikistan[xviii]

Trust and reciprocity often exist *within* but not *between* groups. Power relations can cut across popular self-help mechanisms. It is important not to romanticise traditional forms of connectedness. This case shows how insufficient attention to power can lead NGOs to assume social capital at the local level, leading to some interventions that change less than hoped for.

Hidden power relationships in the village

In an isolated Tajik mountain village an INGO committed to supporting the community's subsistence economy carried out a PRA exercise. The population of 200 families was primarily engaged in herding, supplemented by rain-fed agriculture. The rains are unpredictable and yields of grain are very low, leading to food shortages and hunger. After assessing the situation, the INGO suggested raising sufficient water from the valley below to irrigate 60 hectares of land close to the village, which would guarantee water and mean that all families would have a better harvest. Their feasibility study showed that the whole project, including the pipeline, could be delivered for $130,000. The villagers were enthusiastic and the INGO found a donor.

In preparing the project the INGO made sure that the local authority was willing to issue title deeds to the village. It had no problem with this, agreeing that the land was valueless as it stood and so any improvements should be owned by the villagers. When the project was complete there was a grand celebration attended by a representative of the donor, INGO staff and all the villagers. There was great satisfaction all round. However a few months later the INGO heard that only two land titles had been issued by the local authority and the beneficiaries were two well-known families. Between them they had successfully applied for the entire 60 hectares. By virtue of their status as patrons for the village's traditional feast, they exercised considerable hidden power.

Although the villagers did not complain about the situation, the INGO went to the local authority to remonstrate – after all, the understanding had been that the newly irrigated land would be equally shared between the families and guaranteed by title deeds. However the INGO found that this source of visible power was unrepentant, arguing that the big families always looked after the others in such isolated mountain communities. Fearful of the report that it would have to write to the donor, the INGO took its complaint to the central government. The INGO director was not aware that the biggest family in the village was well-connected with the congressman for the region, who always attended the annual village feast.

The congressman used his power to neutralise the INGO. The INGO found itself the subject of an intensive audit from the Ministry of Finance, which found a mounting series of discrepancies in its financial arrangements. There were even suggestions that the supplier of the pipes had diverted them from a government project. The INGO quickly dropped the case and was eventually able to clear its name.

The two families continue to give the villagers access to the land. However, their access is forever dependent on keeping on good terms with the village leaders, whose power is greatly enhanced. The social capital between local elites, local authorities and even national elites also worked to preserve power in this paternalistic society.

Lessons

'Local communities' are more fractured than suggested by the rhetoric of the development industry. Traditional forms of connectedness can have great bonding strengths for oppressed populations but can have little direct effect on structural injustice and inequalities. It is of utmost importance to analyse power structures within civil society and especially when there are strong interests at play. Local elites everywhere have sophisticated techniques for maintaining their privileges.

A Tajik NGO that witnessed this process commented that INGOs should try as far as possible to analyse hidden power to reveal who may stand to lose as well as benefit from any intervention. First of all, using various participatory methods, the development agency should make sure it thoroughly understands the social structure and relations and identify where different types of power reside in the community. The next stage is to use role play or other modelling methods to explore various options for future ownership of the infrastructure needed to put the land to good use, as well as the resulting profit. Finally the village should devise a transparent system for deciding amongst the options: for example, in this case, mapping the distribution of land between families living in the village.

Recommendations

The cases in this chapter demonstrate the rare, hard earned, but essential nature of social capital, both in horizontal and vertical directions, if effective changes are to be made. This knowledge should be a rallying cry for INGOs to become true supporters of civil society once more, both because CSOs are often already embedded in relationships with strong social capital, and because those networks of trust and reciprocity urgently need to be strengthened, especially in fragile contexts.

1. Recognise the high value of organisations with strong membership bases

If CSOs are to play a constructive role in development, the social capital that comes from having a constituency is essential. Too often INGOs are in competition with local civil society, too risk averse to work with social movements, or they impose funding-led priorities over those coming from a strong membership base. Instead, a core purpose should be supporting CSOs which are formed on the basis of solidarity between members to retain their independence. Capacity building shouldn't create 'clones' but seek to reinforce the competencies of organisations and people to achieve their own goals and to focus on the voices of their particular constituency. Financially, encouraging reliance on membership subscriptions is one important way of doing this. Membership-based organisations also often effectively bridge the service–advocacy divide.

A second point is that people are members of multiple groups and we must resist defining them by only one characteristic, whether this may be ethnicity, religion, trade union membership, political party and so on. Narrow definitions polarise civil society. Rather we should encourage multiple group membership and roles. For example, in a UK context one person may be a mother, a PTA member, a churchwarden, a volunteer at an old people's residential home; and she may work for the government as an auditor, and vote for the Liberal Democrats. The greater the diversity of associational life, the stronger will be social capital and, hence, civil society. One situation where it may be particularly challenging but important to support civil society in its capacity for social capital is in post-conflict situations. Too often civic space in these contexts is filled by local spin-offs of international humanitarian agencies who have funding, but this is not an adequate approach to a diverse civic space which will have the social capital necessary to rebuild their society and prevent further conflict.

2. Recognise the diversity of local channels which can create trust

Social capital is built through diverse channels – from funeral societies to ICT networks. Development practitioners should gain contextual knowledge about existing sources of trust in the society and culture they work, and think outside the box to work with these. Many societies have informal associations linked with the life-cycle, such as the Ethiopian *Iddir* burial societies which not only help families with the costs of mourning and burying their dead, but through small regular contributions also engage in developmental activities that are important to their members: upgrading slum housing, credit and savings schemes, assistance to the elderly and orphans. The *Iddir* includes people from all classes – from the highest government officials to the poorest peasant.[xix]

Faith communities can be an extremely important channel for social capital formation. Throughout the world, churches, mosques and temples provide one of the rare opportunities for rich and poor to congregate as equals. For example in Armenia's transitional, nominally democratic polity, threatened by endemic corruption and tribalism, the Apostolic church, one of the oldest Christian denominations in the world, is one of the only institutions to enjoy public trust. Although generally a very small minority, courageous parts of civil society are sometimes willing to reach out to build trust between one faith group to another, even across lines of conflict. The Pontanima Choir is an inspiring example from former Yugoslavia, as it fractured along ethnic and religious lines. It brings together all the peoples of multi-ethnic Bosnia to sing the sacred music of the Catholic, Eastern Orthodox, Protestant, Muslim and Jewish traditions.

In rural areas, communal work efforts and risk-spreading mechanisms such as share cropping in the commercial sphere, or grain stores, seed banks and irrigation committees, build social capital. The *minga* communal work effort of the Andes, for large one-off tasks, is reinforced by *ayni*, a system of reciprocal labour that makes light of regular agricultural tasks. *Ashar* is a similar system that has been reinvented in Kyrgyzstan to form self-help groups as a means of surviving the economic rigours of transition.

The revolution in global connectedness created by ongoing ICT developments is another key channel. The mobile phone in India is the most dramatic example, as the number of mobile phone connections has expanded exponentially since 2001, to reach 617 million in 2010, around half the 1.2 billion population. On current trends the number of phone connects is expected to cover the entire population in three years. Surprisingly, given that the third of the population living in poverty is mainly rural, most users are outside the major cities. The mobile phone reaches across regions and deep into the villages and slums, and is credited with galvanising small businesses as well as checking on corrupt politics.

3. Treat power relationships between different actors cautiously

Reciprocal relationships and networks are essential in work that aims to support civil society's capacity to build trust, but too often there are more hidden relationships of power than we might be aware of. Critical questions should be asked. Do CSOs have the trust of their own community and its leadership? Do local political parties and central government recognise the importance of non-party CSOs or do they see them as competitors to be co-opted or destroyed? Elite capture of civic space within emerging democracies can provoke uncivil reactions in society, marginalising civil society's non-violent vocation, or simply not effect any change of the defined spaces in which social capital operates.

Whilst power differences will to some extent always remain at the heart of lop-sided development, it is imperative to tackle polarising differences of class, influence and privilege if poverty and inequality are to be sustainably reduced. Peru's government is a case in point, as centuries of social capital formation in traditional communities seemed to be powerless against the financial capital, connections and privileges of elite rulers anxious to benefit from the current oil and mineral bonanza. Central government has opened up great swathes of its remote Andean and Amazon regions, altering the constitution to do so and repressing, or co-opting sovereign social movements. Neighbouring Bolivia presents a counter-argument. For the first time in 500 years, an Indian presides over the republic. As a coca farmer and union representative, Evo Morales has benefited from grassroots connections with the country's *campesino* bedrock. At the end of 2009 he was re-elected with the largest majority ever seen in Bolivian electoral history.

One particularly tricky area for practitioners to be aware of is that of civil society's relationships with the powerful and privileged, whether this means engaging with the government or private sector. It is important to distinguish whether this is for confrontational reasons; or in building partnerships to achieve a common goal, sometimes to lobby for common interests; and occasionally to seek resources from the private sector. Each will require a different way of working and clarity over the aims and strategy to be followed. It is important to consider whether in a particular context, work with the private sector and government will be viewed as a form of cooptation, or whether CSOs need support and encouragement to interact more with some elements of these sectors. Promoting accountability mechanisms for the private sector can be a way of producing trust between these different stakeholders, but CSOs need to ensure that things such as corporate social responsibility initiatives are based on genuinely equal and well negotiated partnerships.

4. Encourage and promote horizontal links and networks between CSOs

External support organisations should help to build networks rather than acting as 'gatekeepers' between various actors within civil society. The activities that will be needed for civil society to increase trust and social capital may look very different under different governance conditions. But whatever is undertaken, supporting the long-term building of participatory decision making relationships at the local level can have lasting effects, and relationships of trust, reciprocity and networks go beyond the existence of particular initiatives. Networks based on equal interaction, such as the movement described in Costa Rica, had a highly valuable effect beyond the particular campaign. Those supporting civil society should emphasise building such relational capacity. Furthermore, they should not artificially keep particular organisations or fora alive for their own sake. Civil society does not need to maintain a permanent, expensive infrastructure in order to express itself. When links of trust and cooperation are there, civil society can mobilise rapidly by using the voluntary social networks that permeate society.

> ## Summary of key points
>
> - Social capital is about reinforcing trust, reciprocity and building networks. These are essential to solve problems and work towards change.
>
> - Strong membership bases for CSOs and social movements mean that they have the trust and solidarity needed to tackle large scale, persistent inequality. Social capital between the oppressed is effective to mobilise for change.
>
> - Producing trust between marginalised people and local authorities at the community level through substantial and strategic participation to bring about change in the way decisions are made is painstaking but rewarding.
>
> - There are diverse channels that can be effective in building social capital at various levels of civil society. In particular, traditional forms of association and new technology both have the potential to facilitate equal and participatory networking. These networks can lead to mutual capacity building, and produce links of trust and capital which enable civil society to rapidly mobilise when needed.
>
> - Where trust has been dramatically undermined, strong sources of social capital, such as faith communities, may be important in beginning to demand reciprocity from government and multinationals. Accountability mechanisms where governments and citizens can begin to engage in good faith are promising bases for restoring relationships of trust and reciprocity between state and citizens.
>
> - INGOs trying to support civil society should not assume strong social capital in the 'local community' and should pay attention to hidden power relationships which may impact their interventions. They should also be attentive to governance conditions and the nuances of whether building social capital will involve advocacy, service provision, or both.

5

Creating and promoting alternatives

Introduction

Whether at the level of ideas or in practice, new concepts, activities, institutions and socio-economic solutions often arise through civil society. The vested interests of politicians and civil servants alike tend to lead to the sluggish development of ideas and services. Therefore the role of civil society in developing ideas, piloting them in practice and lobbying for their adoption is an essential quality of civil society. However, civil society's freedom to evolve ideas can also present challenges to liberal democracy – there are no overarching values shaping what kinds of alternatives civil society creates in different contexts. Rather, different ideas about alternatives compete with each other. Some of these will be incompatible and require negotiation across and within civil society as well as with the state and market. The challenge for civil society groups is whether they can gain legitimacy for their new concepts.

📖 Theoretical background

While the emphasis is usually placed on the role of civil society in promoting liberal values, it more closely resembles a public battleground of alternative ideas, of which some are better or 'more liberal' than others. Antonio Gramsci, the early 20th century Italian Marxist, developed a theory of 'cultural hegemony' to explain why the working classes fail to rise up against the bourgeoisie. Simply put, Gramsci explained that civil society becomes complacent in the face of exploitation by absorbing the values of the ruling class as 'common sense'. The emancipation of the working classes from their bondage, argued Gramsci, required a fight over dominant, or 'hegemonic', ideas as a precursor to their mobilisation against the ruling classes.

Gramsci's insight into the complexity of civil society remains relevant today. Elements of civil society have, for example, supported authoritarian and oppressive regimes, such as Pinochet's Chile. Perhaps the contribution to development of civil society can be determined by the extent to which actors and organisations within it promote viable 'alternatives' to dominant thinking. Scholars are increasingly returning to Gramsci's ambivalent characterisation of civil society as constituting an 'arena in which hegemonic ideas concerning the organisation of social and economic life are both established and contested'.[xx]

This chapter shows civil society innovations and alternatives to:
- traditional patterns of ownership and power
- the challenges of conflict
- supporting livelihoods
- influencing policy and legislation.

In each of the cases, the initiatives demonstrate fulfilment of the other functions of civil society outlined in other chapters, building the social basis for democracy, promoting political accountability, producing trust, reciprocity and networks, and supporting the rights and concept of citizenship. The driving force behind the first two cases in this section is equity – the universal rights of the homeless and the landless to shelter and livelihood, applied to specific contexts in Bangladesh and Buenos Aires. The ideas they apply in action move from the margins of social protest to mainstream cooperation with local government. The novelty in Bangladesh is transparency and participation in the distribution of government lands to the landless; in Argentina the homeless resolve the chronic housing shortage by planning and carrying out their own urban redevelopment project. Quality of process and an emphasis on cooperation are central to their innovation.

The third case in Sri Lanka shows the challenging search for alternatives in situations of conflict. A new INGO develops a niche in supporting local civil society peace activists through 'unarmed accompaniment'. However, the case also introduces the indication that this function of civil society can easily slip away, as the pressure for growth risks making the INGO rapidly indistinguishable from global humanitarian organisations. On the other hand, civil society at its best can be highly creative in responding to challenges through innovative new approaches and in utilising new technology. The fourth case outlines how telecentres have produced results in Kerala, helping farmers to visualise good practice from distant villages and communicate directly with researchers. The fifth case explores how an ambitious and eventually successful attempt to have the African Union adopt positive legislation for women's rights owes more to old-fashioned networking and lobbying than ICT. This demonstrates the important point that civil society's capacity to create and promote alternatives does not always mean applying new methods but in thinking outside the box and being willing to try new approaches in search of the most effective solutions.

Case studies

5.1 Dying for the right to own land in Bangladesh

To be landless in agricultural Bangladesh condemns families to abject poverty. Despite a seemingly well developed rights regime, justice and equity are novelties rather than the norm. Movements for the landless need courage in order to face down the landowners' thugs. They also require creativity to convince government and public opinion to take their side.

In overpopulated south-west Bangladesh there is a well-established policy for distributing government-owned agricultural land to the poor and landless on a priority basis. However, in practice this all too rarely happens because of fierce competition over land, mainly from wealthy and powerful community members who want to farm shrimps and earn a slice of the profits from the country's second most important export industry after clothing. Corrupt government officials and local police often side with the shrimp farmers, leading to periodic confrontations between officials and villagers, which have led to a significant number of villagers' deaths.

'Uttaran' is a local NGO working in the south-western Satkhira District since 1985. Led by Shahidul Islam, a leading human rights defender on land, water and river issues, over the years it gradually helped villagers build up a powerful right to land movement. On a single day in July 1998 the movement was crushed by an overwhelming force of gunmen and police sent to evict villagers from the government lands they had been settled on for years. Altogether 265 houses were looted and burned, 229 people were shot and wounded and a woman leader of the movement was killed.

The movement's leaders were rounded up in order to prevent resistance, but the NGO gave emergency support to the survivors and helped mobilise fresh leaders. These organised a strike by the landless that brought the entire district to a standstill for a week. When it turned out that the eviction order was based on forged title deeds, central government became alarmed. The Prime Minister visited, expressed support for the landless and ordered a task force to be set up under the Minister for Land to solve the problem. The task force made a start by drawing up a list of all landless people and an inventory of available government land.

Uttaran seized the opportunity to push for a comprehensive solution to landlessness. First it organised the movement's membership of 28,000 into small groups and raised funds for their training and campaigning activities. Next it linked these groups with the Union Parishads, the lowest tier of government, within a Land Committee. Over the following years Uttaran helped the Land Committee develop and implement a public sector land settlement programme.

Innovations
This was a breakthrough in civil society–local government cooperation: a coming to terms of former opponents in order to right a long-standing wrong inflicted by the wealthy upon the poor with the connivance of the government. From the basis of direct action, organisation of members and the formation of a new civil society alliance in the form of the Land Committee, an alternative to the previous, deeply unjust status quo was built. Uttaran's other innovations include developing a participatory model for matching landless families with appropriate government land using transparent and democratic methods – no more old-style negotiations behind closed doors between landlords and officials.

The basis of the new model was the public hearing held by civil society committees at Ward and Union levels. These committees oversaw the distribution process and were made up of a broad membership, including trusted individuals such as religious leaders and teachers, cooperative officials, and NGO and political party representatives. Cases submitted to the committees were backed up by a process that ensured everyone was included – for example drawings, songs and theatre were used to make sure the illiterate were able to understand what was going on. Although the problem of landlessness is far from solved in Bangladesh, by September 2008 nearly 9,000 landless people had received over 6,500 acres of government land.

Lessons

Social movements often regard human rights NGOs as birds of passage, flying in and out of remote areas according to their own seasons and interests. However, this NGO had developed trusting relationships with the landless people's movement through being deeply rooted in the locality, which enabled it to take a courageous role in seeking alternatives. When the local authorities needed a way out of the social unrest created by the old way of doing things, they also turned to the NGO. The NGO's careful positioning enabled them to shift from a confrontational to a cooperative approach with the state as the occasion demanded, and thus promote a new, more transparent and equitable way of making decisions about land in the district.

5.2 Community-led housing in Buenos Aires

Local authorities have the mandate and resources to resolve social problems. But they are often rigidly structured and find it hard to think 'outside the box'. In Argentina it took trade union activists to make the connection between unemployment and scarce public housing. By linking these serious urban problems creatively, they established a new model which met the need for jobs and houses.

At the millennium, over half of Argentina's population of 37 million was living in poverty, and only three out of four workers were able to find a job. The unemployed were getting welfare, but no retraining to improve their chances of future work opportunities. Four years of recession had also forced the government to cut back on construction and by 2008 a serious deficit of affordable housing had arisen. There was a real need for new ideas to tackle these two issues of housing and jobs.

The Territorial Liberation Movement (TLM) is an Argentina-wide workers' movement that attributes its members' difficulties to the privatisation and free trade policies of the 1990s. As its name implies, the TLM at first used radical means to force the government to change direction. It occupied buildings and staged roadblocks on major highways, demanding jobs and housing and denouncing evictions and corruption. Over time TLM became more pragmatic, and began to develop innovative projects that offered its members employment opportunities at the same time as housing and community facilities.

In creating alternative solutions to the housing and employment shortage the movement used a crucial regulation that pro-worker CSOs, including TLM, had long lobbied for. Law 341 of the Buenos Aires municipal housing institute was passed in 2000, allowing community based organisations that register as cooperatives to receive public funds for self-managed housing construction. TLM took its first loan under Law 341 in 2003, to provide housing for 326 families. The movement also set up the Emetele housing cooperative to execute the project with technical support from TLM's professionals.

Do-it-yourself community housing

The Monteagudo Complex is a model project for homeless families with no access to credit. A disused paint factory was converted into housing, rather than being demolished. There were challenges faced in strengthening the foundations and making the building safe for residential use. But these were overcome and the unit now consists of 10 one-storey buildings with a choice of one, two and three bedroom units. As well as the housing, the complex includes shops, a day nursery, communal areas, a community radio and a training centre.

Combining loans and grants (for the communal facilities), the job was done in just 30 months at a fraction of the cost of traditional social housing. The residents, mostly refugees or foreign migrants from neighbouring republics, did all the work themselves, having received training in the centre. Some of the residents were long-term unemployed and had lost the will to work; but the on-site training centre helped them find new motivation which had impact beyond the project. Altogether 400 workers found jobs after they had built their own homes and with their new salaries they would pay back their loans. Since then the Emetele Cooperative registered as a construction company and has built 700 more housing units across the city.

This was the first community led and community managed housing project in the country. It received a great deal of press attention and was replicated by CBOs from far afield, with many still visiting the project for inspiration.

Lessons

The project used an imaginative approach, working from the base of progressive legislation to create an alternative that made a significant impact on addressing two problems: a lack of social housing and long-term unemployment. Public housing does not have to be poor quality in construction and design. Nor does it have to be contracted out to the private sector. The social and community benefits gained by such community-led housing projects should encourage other civil society groups to do it themselves. In many developed and developing countries there are backlogs in social housing and residents are often alienated by standardised, low quality provision. The alternative solution here arose from civil society, and has potential to be replicated.

5.3 Protecting civilians in Sri Lanka

Civil wars cry out for imaginative civil responses. Hostilities in these extreme man-made emergencies are rarely as clearcut on the ground as they are between the main contenders. Activists need to work for peaceful solutions before, during and after their communities are engulfed. In certain circumstances the presence of neutral, outside 'accompaniers' can provide security in these extremely hazardous encounters and facilitate community level organisations' work for peace.

The stresses and tensions that build up in communities overwhelmed by conflict often prevent local CSOs, even when they are human rights or peace-orientated, from carrying out their missions. Unarmed protection is a strategy developed over the last 25 years for these situations. A relatively new arrival on the humanitarian scene, it enables trained civilians to support other civilians who work for peace in the midst of violent conflict, using nonviolent conflict resolution methods. The reasoning is that long-term, high-level peace agreements are not enough on their own, rather peace is only sustainable with the support of civil society.

Peacekeeping and violence prevention in Sri Lanka

Founded by US activists in 2002, Nonviolent Peaceforce (NP) is a rapidly growing INGO with 80 staff from 20 countries. It claims to be the world's only paid and trained unarmed civilian peacekeeping force, and not only works to establish dialogue among conflicting groups, but also incorporates innovative strategies to protect civilians.

NP launched its first joint project in Sri Lanka in 2003, at the invitation of several local and national Sri Lankan peace organisations. The aim of the project was to increase the safety of civilians in the 20-year-old civil war, to contribute to lasting peace with justice. The objectives were to build the confidence of local organisations, provide space for networks to function at community level and facilitate coordinated action for security.

Working in Jaffna in the North and Trincomalee and Batticalao in the East, one innovative approach that NP used was to provide unarmed accompaniment by trained internationals for women searching for their forcibly recruited children, or for NGO partners carrying out community awareness programmes, or even Buddhist monks fearful of armed groups.

NP also supported Peace Committees aimed at bringing different communities together to discuss early signs of communal tensions and other issues. When violence erupted and hundreds of families sought refuge in churches, temples or mosques, NP was able to visit the makeshift camps and convey their needs to other humanitarian agencies. The work of NP in identifying and supporting strong community networks in part prevented the same violence from spreading. For example, the Valaichenai Traders Association, made up of Tamil and Muslim businesses, asked NP to host a meeting in which 30 traders came together to discuss preventive measures.

NP's teams in Jaffna and Colombo also supported the local human rights community during conflict, and post-conflict. They tried to create opportunities for human rights defenders from the North and East to increase their capacity and network with others doing difficult human rights work in their own areas. The official government Human Rights Commission would also call for NP's presence and accompaniment during field investigations, including contested border areas where land disputes can quickly turn violent.

By 2008 NP had 50 staff working in five locations in Sri Lanka. Following the end of the civil war in May 2009, the organisation started a series of longer term recovery initiatives, training the human rights CSOs it had cooperated with during the hostilities and broadening their mandate to implement protection programmes in the camps of displaced people. NP has a new headquarters in Brussels and plans to field 300 peacekeepers by 2012.

Lessons

New organisations working in the crowded field of man-made humanitarian emergencies face the challenge of defining a new mission and keeping to it. Since a focus on civil society is often lacking in conflict situations, innovation such as NP's unarmed accompaniment is always welcome. Their enabling work supported peace building at the local level, but now the demands of organisational growth have moved them into a broader mandate which may possibly risk displacing the original intentions of civilian cooperation for peace.

5.4 Using telecentres to share farming expertise in South India

There have been countless mutations of efforts in the developing world to improve the agricultural productivity and livings of poor farmers. However, efforts seem to constantly encounter challenges, and rural poverty remains stubbornly persistent. Can information and communication technology (ICT) make the difference by linking researchers directly with the farmers they serve?

ICT can play a major role in improving knowledge transfer in small-scale agriculture. The experience of the Rural Agency for Social and Technological Advancement (RASTA) in Kerala, India, shows that farmers are keen to use online communications, information and videos to learn from each other about farming. Using new technology to bring together information on new methods has provided an alternative and highly effective way of helping poor farmers improve their livelihoods.

People have their own solutions

Kerala, one of the southernmost Indian states, is populated mainly by people who make their living from agriculture, either as producers or as farm labourers. Farming mainly used to be subsistence crops, but agriculture has become more market oriented in the past 50 years. Now, farmers grow spices, coffee and fruit for sale in addition to paddy rice. People have neglected soil and water conservation and at the same time agriculture has become more intensive with the increasing use of pesticides and fertilisers. This has created water shortages, deforestation and environmental problems in Kerala. In 2004 there was an agricultural crisis when these environmental problems were compounded by falling prices for crops, job losses, and pest attacks.

RASTA has worked with Keralan women for 25 years. It runs thrift and savings groups and self-help groups for women. Self-help groups (SHGs) are groups of 10-12 women who meet each week to mobilise savings and discuss their plans. Over time, a strong leadership and sense of collective action evolves among group members and this collective strength is often guided towards starting new or alternative livelihood activities. RASTA has found that the self-help group approach is highly effective for empowering women and finding appropriate livelihood activities. Since agriculture, the primary livelihood sector, was facing a crisis, RASTA has placed much emphasis encouraging SHGs to get involved in initiatives such as training farmers in sustainable agriculture production systems, knowledge sharing, field extension services and diversification of crops.

Agricultural knowledge transfer

RASTA has supported agricultural knowledge transfer for over twenty years and has learnt the importance of collective farmer-to-farmer learning for improving agriculture. One of the major problems is that farmers often receive biased information from fertiliser sales people and others, whose advice focuses on selling products rather than supporting sustainability.

To counteract this, RASTA set up a Village Knowledge Centre in 2004, run by the local women's SHGs. This centre holds documentation of successful sustainable farming practices, both traditional and modern, that RASTA has collected over the years. Even though farmers have traditional knowledge and receive some information from the media, they were not satisfied with the information available before the establishment of these centres.

Farmers also look for practical information on issues such as the market for their crops, solving pest and disease issues, and livestock management. Many farmers request information on selling their crops as they are often unaware of the market prices – they are at the mercy of the wholesale dealers who buy for low prices. This is very important in a region were the majority of the crops cultivated are cash crops.

So in 2006, RASTA upgraded the knowledge centre into a telecentre. The state of Kerala is very supportive of exposing the population to the benefits of technology, and the Ministry of Agriculture has set up similar information and networking platforms – but not at the village level. Thanks to an EU-funded project, RASTA could involve the local women's federation in setting up the telecentre.

From the field to the net

A telecentre is a public place where people can access a variety of communication services. The centres are equipped with computers with internet access and telephone facilities. They focus on facilitating knowledge exchange between farmers, community groups, research institutes and intermediary organisations. In this way, farmers can ask questions from agricultural experts in research institutes. The questions are translated into English by the telecentre operator and emailed to the expert. Farmers can also phone experts directly.

The information available comes from both local and research sources. Good practices in agriculture are collected from the villagers, farmers, experts, and research institutions. These good practices are documented systematically and stored in the telecentre database. The tools at the telecentre include a website (see www.farmfriend.org), a online database of examples, including videos of good agricultural practice, and an online discussion forum.

An important aspect of the telecentre is that the information is made available in the local language (Malayalam), referring to local conditions and crops. The video clips of good practice – made by a team of five local women – are a particularly popular way to disseminate knowledge. Farmers are most interested in viewing the videos and replicating the practices.

The results of setting up telecentres for agricultural information are significant: there has been a sudden shift in the ways that the farmers, especially women, look at agriculture. Many of the technologies illustrated through videos and text have been replicated by local women farmers. One advantage is that the information is available in their village and that it is visual. There are many cases where women agriculturalists have learnt and applied new composting methods through the telecentre – not only in Kerala, but as far afield as West Bengal, thousands of kilometres away.

Lessons

The case shows that where there is local ownership of local information, new technology can be used in highly effective ways to share knowledge that improves livelihoods. The experiences from RASTA in Kerala shows that community-run telecentres can bridge the information and knowledge gap in regards to agriculture, provided it is supported by a good content development team and a pool of experts. Providing content in local languages and using video clips are excellent communication tools. Community ownership and not-profit ways of working ensure the sustainability of the centre. One favourable factor in these areas is strong women's self-help groups, which have catalysed the successful implementation of the project activities.

5.5 Women's rights in Africa: ICT or 'beyond the electronic'?

Sequestered in their spanking new complex in Addis Ababa, officials of the African Union (AU) soon found something else was needed to bring the inter-governmental body to life. The missing element was civil society, and activists did not wait to be invited. By keeping officials in touch with grassroots thinking across Africa, civil society organisations are trying to ensure that the Union can be a progressive standard-setter.

In 2003, the AU adopted a continent-wide Protocol on the Rights of Women that held out the promise of fundamental improvements in women's lives – including the rights to social protection, inheritance of property, the banning of female genital mutilation and many other elements. The problem with the Protocol was that it would only enter into force once 15 African nations ratified it, and only then could the task of making change happen at national and local levels begin.

When it became apparent the following year that nations were being slow to ratify the protocol, a group of 29 women's organisations formed Solidarity for African Women's Rights (SOAWR) in order to advocate for states to ratify, implement and popularise the Protocol. SOAWR was to achieve this by working alongside the AU, explicitly using ICT.

The social justice network Fahamu supported the effort through its 'Pambazuka News'. This online platform for CSOs had started in 2000 as an email newsletter and by 2004 had over half a million hits a week. 'Pambazuka', which means 'Arise' in KiSwahili, linked SOAWR members to a continental community of potential support. AU representatives also drew their information on the protocol from the Pambazuka News, as well as from other Fahamu publications and so were better informed when SOAWR lobbyists made contact.

SOAWR realised that a more popular approach was needed to bring the Protocol within reach of communities. The vast bulk of the people who could be positively impacted by the Protocol lie beyond the range of the internet, and have little understanding of the legalese in which the Protocol was composed. Pambazuka editor, Firoze Manji, argued they would have to 'go beyond the electronic' if they ever wanted to have grassroots impact. To put this into practice, SOAWR and Fahamu created a radio drama series for use by community radio and organisations working on women's rights issues, and crucially, also began intensifying their lobbying efforts at the AU.

The Protocol entered into force in November 2005 with the 15th ratification and by mid-2009 stood at 27 signatories – half of the AU's current membership of 54 states. Recent research suggests that although the online and offline work was helpful in raising the profile of SOAWR and the Protocol, the key was the relationships built by SOAWR lobbyists at the AU and with officials from the member states.

The relationships built by SOAWR lobbyists gained them recognition as 'players in their own right' both collectively and individually, resulting in invitations to join meetings and working groups – even AU posts: the Special Rapporteur on Women's Rights, Soyata Maïga is herself the former director of a SOAWR organisation. She frequently updates SOAWR members on what is going on with the Protocol at the AU and has asked for their help, claiming that she needs civil society's assistance to do her job effectively.

Lessons
Almost by definition innovative thinking and strategy lie behind every successful social change campaign. The key lesson here is that innovative use of media and ICT, though important, do not necessarily replace age-old methods of lobbying and relationship building. Isolated in their headquarters, AU officials needed direct contact with civil society representatives at a high level to convince them of the need to ratify the women's rights protocol. In this respect, gaining access to political spaces not normally open to civil society has been the most important aspect of the campaign – even if SOAWR acknowledges that ratification of the Protocol was the easiest part of their job compared to implementation.

Recommendations

It is easy to fall into supporting the status quo, and these cases send a clear message to INGOs that to support civil society to thrive in its ability to create and promote alternative solutions to poverty and suffering, they cannot merely stick to their default ways of doing things. INGOs need to adopt a much more explicit focus on strengthening civil society and implement strategies which foster its innovatory capacities.

1. It is time to throw out the 'sacred cow' of scale and replicability
The function of creating and promoting alternatives is not about going to scale – it is about exploring what works, through piloting new ideas, and exiting once projects work. The norm in development is to scale up when things seem to work; the larger the scale the better, for more impact and lower transaction costs. But innovation within civil society bows to values of its own, with only a passing nod to the separate logics of market and state. For example the driving force behind the first two cases in this section is equity – the universal

rights of the homeless and the landless to shelter and livelihood. Both cases go to scale, but the journey is essentially about equitable solutions driven from the margins of social protest to cooperation with local government. Scale can also be part of northern dominance – but exchange of new ideas must be equal, not imposed. Ideas need to be analysed and debated in local contexts by local actors and, dependent on the outcome of these debates, some may be adopted and replicated, whilst others may have a much more limited scope.

CSOs need to break free of the self-imposed tyranny of carving out a new 'sector' or area of work and entrenching ourselves there. Scaling up is better left to other actors in society: entrepreneurs in the marketplace, providers of common goods in the public sector, and policy makers within the domain of democratic governance. In the quest for new ways of dealing with old problems, less is often more and bigger is not necessarily better.

2. We should put a premium on risk and experiments

INGOs in particular have become risk averse, some suggest even too conservative to recognise and support innovation in comparison to business start-ups in the market sector. They have grown 'too big to fail' and yet it is precisely through failing that learning opportunities and resilience for innovation can arise. Small- and large-scale experiments should be encouraged. However, we should not romanticise the capacity of civil society to be innovative, rather, CSOs face many barriers to innovation. One of these can be an ironic lack of application of the values they espouse for others within their own organisations, such as the issue of gender in leadership, and the adoption of private sector values and operational methods over the very mission of the organisation.[xxi] The Sri Lanka case shows that innovatory approaches such as 'unarmed accompaniment' can be swallowed by the pressure for growth on the parent organisation, which risks becoming rapidly indistinguishable from global humanitarian INGOs. There is an urgent need for strategic donor funding to support a climate of new thinking, practice and learning within civil society.

3. The sector needs to develop a new range of management tools suitable to fostering innovation

Performance management is designed for measuring large-scale service provision. Its obsession with targets, efficiency and effectiveness has spread from the public sector to the aid industry, as a way of catering for accountability demands in major donor-funded programmes. Although it has become an aid industry standard for all types of programming, not just service delivery, performance management is unsuitable for planning and assessing the type of civic sector innovation discussed here.

To foster civil society's capacity for innovation, the direction of accountability needs to be turned on its head, with the constituency calling the shots, rather than the donor or the implementing agency. Criteria of assessment need to switch to outcomes and impact, using indicators to capture change in degrees of 'civic-ness' with due attention to the quality of the process. Engagement, empowerment and participation become outputs and outcomes in themselves.

4. Progressive civil society must critique dominant aid industry paradigms

Civil society is a space for contesting different ideas, demands and approaches. We should celebrate, not be shocked by, this diversity. The work of theorists like Gramsci indicates that we should not to be complacent about the uses and abuses of civil society. In the right circumstances, certain parts of it can help build the social basis for democracy, promote political accountability, produce social trust and support citizens' rights. However, often civil society serves the interests of the establishment, reinforcing systems for maintaining power and marginalising discordant voices. Usually this takes place by co-opting them and their ideas, but can also occur more drastically – through starving them of funds, banning or criminalising them.

CSOs can, and often do, represent these mainstream views – often without realising it. Well-endowed think tanks articulate agenda-setting policy slogans such as 'small government', 'free trade', and 'popular participation'. However, INGOs that work from these agendas are widely seen in the civil societies of the South as instruments of globalisation, having greatly benefited from the roll-back of the state, at least in terms of financial growth and geographical expansion. At worst, some have surrendered the capacity to contest self-serving western policies on debt, trade, development, governance, investment conditions and others. All this goes to say that to fulfil their innovating role adequately, progressive CSOs can and must articulate critiques of the dominant development paradigm and present alternatives to it. Failure to challenge hegemonic thinking has exposed civil society actors to persistent criticism of ineffectiveness.[xxii]

Innovation can sometimes mean an embrace of the new, but equally importantly, means being courageous enough to try various solutions, and committed enough to choose the most effective. For instance, the use of ICT in telecentres has produced results in Kerala, helping farmers to visualise good practice from distant villages and communicate directly with researchers. But equally, even after a quality ICT campaign, those working for the African Union to adopt positive legislation for women's rights felt that to get the best results they needed to go back to 'beyond online', with community awareness raising and face-to-face networking and lobbying.

We have lived through a generation of false and often unsuccessful development fads which should give us more confidence to be able to challenge the next poorly thought out idea masquerading as serious policy. Kumi Naidoo, at the INTRAC 2008 conference, pleaded for more attention to justice, equality and power – words that should be at the heart of progressive civil society practice. Don't be afraid to argue a minority case that is based on values, rather than the status quo, and be clear when the 'emperor's new clothes' don't consist of much at all.

Summary of key points

 An essential role of civil society lies in developing ideas, piloting them in practice and lobbying for their adoption, though there is always a struggle over which alternatives are accepted as legitimate.

 A powerful driving force behind civil society's promotion of alternatives is equity and universal rights. Innovations take shape by moving from the margins of social protest to mainstream cooperation with local government.

 New technology and ICT can be a powerful, highly effective tool for innovative solutions. Where there is local ownership of local information, the knowledge transfer potential of new technology can improve livelihoods.

 Equally, sometimes innovation is about having the courage to try and test different solutions, and finding what is most effective to address the particular problem, whether that method is old or new, fashionable or out of favour.

 Alternatives are easily subsumed and watered down by the larger status quo: there must be a strategic emphasis on fostering experimentation.

 INGOs must encourage both CSOs and themselves to think critically, and have the courage to experiment, rather than getting boxed in by the emphasis on scale, replicability, donor-accountable performance management, and the currently dominant development slogans.

6

Supporting the rights of citizens and the concept of citizenship

Introduction

The state has to earn its legitimacy from its citizens. The concept of citizens having equal rights politically, and before the law, in access to the services of the state, is basic to democratic conventions. Although in recent years development actors have understood these ideas through 'rights-based approaches', the idea of a contract between the state and citizen is much older. The idea is that a state earns its legitimacy through fulfilling certain obligations to the citizens who live in its territory. Building on this, 'citizenship' is a term which indicates how people within a society undertake activities to claim their constitutional rights. Multiple and overlapping citizen interests are represented by civil society, as organisations lobby for specific interests, services, legal and other protections from the state. In return the citizen and civil society accept the legitimacy of the state. We see many areas of the world where the state is holding onto power by violence, and losing legitimacy with its population, which is unable to access services. Examples include: remote tribal areas of Pakistan which reject the central government; or Somalia, lacking viable government; and the Democratic Republic of Congo, torn apart by competing military groups. In contrast to these often violent expressions of 'uncivil society', others come together in associations of citizens, as civil society, to protect and realise the equal rights of citizens proclaimed by constitutions, either by claiming rights at a universal level but also for specific interests.

It is worth noting here that there is an unresolved debate between those who see citizenship as being a western focus on the individual, and others who look at citizenship through the lens of collective social, economic and cultural rights. The latter are critical of some concepts of rights and democracy as overly concerned with the individual at the expense of the collective. The cases in this chapter should demonstrate that our focus on civil society leads to somewhat of a middle line, given that civil society is about collective associations constituted by individuals who have both rights and responsibilities within them.

> **Theoretical background**
>
> The idea of the citizen can be traced back at least to the Greek concept of democracy according to which citizens met to govern the city state, even though only a limited number of the population were full citizens. In Appendix 2 we describe various ideas about the contract between the state and the citizen. In the early ideas of Hobbes, the state governed on a contract with the citizen but once the state or sovereign was installed, there was little accountability to the citizen or redress by the citizen. Locke and Bentham elaborated ideas around the state being accountable to the citizen, which once accepted provided the legitimacy for the collective action of the citizenry. Civil society is made up of citizens coming together to exercise their individual rights collectively.
>
> Subordinate groups often begin by claiming particular social and economic rights - to 'improve their lot', but often expand to encompass calls for citizen rights more broadly. Foweraker and Landman note that 'because the initial demands can rarely be satisfied in their entirety, and are often restricted, repressed, reversed, or delayed, they frequently generate further demands which have to do with the civil and political conditions of putting demands and making claims; and these demands are more directly legal and political in content'.[xxiii] Ultimately, social movements and civil society organisations develop alliances with other groups to forge collective struggles featuring the language of rights. Thus, the state exists in a symbiotic relationship with citizens and civil society. Social movement theorists recognise that struggles for citizenship legitimise the state as the legal duty-bearer for providing rights. In recent years there has arguably been some movement towards the citizen as an individual consumer of state services rather than the citizen as master of the state.

These case studies focus on how civil society in various contexts has been actively promoting the rights of citizens at different levels. These range from the level of individual citizen's participation in demand for civil rights, to issues facing the civil society sector as a whole in its relations with the state and the market. The first case looks at how the coordinating body for the civic sector in Nicaragua has to expend energy to defend constitutional rights to participation in politics and policy making which are being eroded by a government bent on occupying the civic space itself. From the perspective of supporting the rights of citizens and the concept of citizenship, the ruling Sandinistas have misread the roles of government and society, by trying to monopolise the public arena of debate. This can only lead them down the authoritarian road, resisted by CSOs at every step. Nicaragua has all the makings of yet another state that loses its legitimacy by challenging its own society, initially confronting the progressive elements of civil society and later broader segments.

The second case, from Peru, addresses the theme of activism amongst citizens with HIV/AIDS. This case explores the perspective of the individual citizen when confronting their marginalised position in society and their difficulty in accessing necessary services from the government. Individual citizens go through a process whereby gathering with others to seek personal support provides a space to learn the skills of association and participation which, combined with a sense of urgency, brings them into more direct citizen activism in the public sphere, demanding that the state fulfil its obligations to them as equal citizens. Although this case focuses on the particular challenges of those with HIV/AIDS, many of the lessons will be relevant for encouraging civic participation with other groups.

In the third case we look again at the broad level of civil society as a whole, in Central America, where various civic actors are challenging liberalising governments that see their countries' future in closer ties with the dominant economy of the North. The paramount issue for civil society is the collective social, economic and cultural rights of citizens. Success for civil society here depends on the capacity to tackle regional themes in a new way. Building the connectedness of civil society across the region and its increasing its ability to come up with viable alternatives is a difficult task for donors and INGOs looking to design programmes. This is especially true when the think-tanks and universities that can frame alternatives inhabit very different parts of civil society from its activists.

The final case arises from the context of the increasingly radicalised ethnic movements of South America, which are socially excluded and face discrimination. In both regions, elements in the political establishment have long been reluctant to acknowledge the rights of indigenous peoples to full citizenship and are willing to flout international human rights conventions to deprive them of their resource-rich territories without consultation. In 2009 tensions erupted bloodily between the Peruvian government and the Awajún (sometimes known as the Aguaruna), a hunting people of the country's northern Amazon region, over the sale of their territory in concession to foreign oil companies. Having refused to consult the Awajún, the President made matters worse by describing the country's forest inhabitants as 'second class citizens'.

Case studies

6.1 Civil society seen as a competitor by the state

Civil society in Nicaragua takes the opportunity to engage in 'small p' politics because citizens have the constitutional right to organise and engage in public matters. Coordinadora Civil (CC), a civil society umbrella body, has grown accustomed to taking an active role in policy as well as in service delivery, but find that their practical application of citizenship is being seen as threatening by the state.

The Sandinista government has started to see CSOs as unwelcome competitors for popular support and foreign development funds. The Sandinistas were once a progressive party, but have since adopted policies that set them against their former constituency – the poor and marginalised. The government has also disregarded civil society's constitutional rights by manipulating the structures for engagement between state and society. In this regard they are going in the direction of authoritarian rulers who are uncomfortable with the independent mobilisation of civic actors, distrusting any initiative that originates from outside the government. They seem not to accept the concept of a two-way contract whereby the state is subservient to civil society.

Civil society mobilisation: from Hurricane Mitch to political engagement
Reconstruction efforts in the aftermath of Hurricane Mitch in October 1988 led to the emergence of an organised civil society with renewed self-confidence. In response to government incapacity, citizens' organisations came together to respond to the emergency. The CSOs accessed external funds and cooperated with government institutions to help reach the affected citizens and regions.

The Coordinadora Civil (CC) was created by non-profit and non-partisan citizens' organisations such as NGOs, guilds, trade unions and church groups for better coordination of the massive relief operation. CC's activities soon moved beyond hurricane relief and reconstruction. For example, it conducted a comprehensive social audit of the government's use of foreign emergency funds, including a survey of the effectiveness and transparency of the aid people had received. The survey findings were widely published and the government's lack of concern for the population's basic needs left it open to criticism.

This led to a clash between civil society and officials, but in spite of the government's attempts to sideline CSOs and monopolise the available funds, CSOs were able to survive, and to neutralise these attacks. Through struggling with the government, civil society emerged more invigorated and with a strong sense of unity from having worked together in the emergency, and from having collectively faced threats from the government. Over the following years CC became the focal point for its diverse membership's united goal of influencing public policies by building up a strong citizenship and generating conviction and consensus.

Growing awareness of the importance of a collective civic identity led a group of CSOs to draft a law guaranteeing citizens' participation in the political decisions of the country. In 2003 the National Assembly approved the new law since it reflected the constitutional provision for citizens to 'participate in public matters and in the management of the State'.

Authoritarian tendencies restrict civil society
However in 2007, the year after the new President took office, a cooperation council set up by the previous President was restructured to exclude the most vocal CSOs. The council had benefited from the independent voice of civil society, but under the new rules only those CSOs with Sandinista affiliation, or those content to simply provide services, were welcome.

Coordinadora Civil has a strong track record of political comment and engagement. Its outspoken criticism of neoliberal policies has provoked a confrontation with the current government, which wanted civil society to align itself with the pro-business goals of the Party and to that end wished to suppress different views. For example, the semi-official media accuses civil society of being allied with international forces to discredit and destabilise the Nicaraguan government. One piece of 'strong proof' that the government claimed showed that Coordinadora Civil was a dangerous anti-government force was their use of the slogan 'Democracy, YES; Dictatorship, NO' in marches.

Coordinadora Civil and civil society generally are now treated as dangerous enemies of the state. Meanwhile, wealthy investors are appointed as official 'people's advisers' to influential 'Enterprise Councils', and violent gangs who suppress protests against election fraud have been armed and named patriotic 'Sandinista Activists'. There is real cause for concern that the regime in Nicaragua will become more authoritarian, in disregard of the norms of democracy clearly set out in Nicaragua's Constitution and in the Law of Citizens' Participation.

The case clearly demonstrates the tendency of previously progressive forces to become conservative when in power. Once credited with toppling the most illiberal bastion of Central American politics in the 1970s, the Sandinista party reappeared on a neoliberal platform. This time it ranged itself opposite the popular social movements that had campaigned vigorously against free trade with the USA, and became within two decades an aggressive competitor to progressive elements in civil society. The Sandinistas counter that the CSO network is essentially a group of NGOs financed from the US, with an agenda to subvert the real popular movement represented by the democratically-elected Sandinistas. By August 2009 the dispute between the CC and the Sandinistas had turned violent. More than 21 participants attending the CC's annual assembly in Managua were injured by a mob of 200 people.[xxiv]

Lessons

Successful states need independent civil societies that are free to generate ideas and actions for the public good. In turn, vibrant civil societies need tolerant governments that are strong enough to guarantee civil society's democratic rights. However, many states do not support citizenship in this way. This case shows that those who want to support civil society must be alert to the all too frequent desire of many governments to occupy the civic space themselves, pushing out any dissident voices. Civil society in Nicaragua is resisting this attempt to undermine the constitutional right to participate in politics and to shape policy, but is becoming considered dangerous by a government with increasingly authoritarian tendencies. That said, even fully democratic governments have a tendency to regard civil society as a convenient means of implementing their programmes, and so favour CSOs with the same policy as themselves over other more critical voices.

6.2 Activism by citizens with HIV/AIDS in Peru

How do marginalised groups in society, such as people living with HIV/AIDS (PLHA), feel about their possibilities for citizenship and participation? Research for the Global Fund in Peru helped to provide insights into the possibilities and challenges for full citizenship and participation for PLHA, which are relevant to supporting civic engagement of many marginalised groups.

Research in Lima took place with the main networks of PLHA and different actors related to CONAMUSA, the Ministry of Health coordinating body that brings together government, civil society and donors. Focus groups and participatory techniques were used in order to help the activists tell their stories. Activists drew 'The river of my participation', sharing stories of political awareness and their relationship with their personal experiences through using the metaphors of waterfalls, eddies, tributaries and stones. They also expressed how they experienced their participation in CONAMUSA through different images. Two key ideas emerged during the research.

'Necessity participation' of the marginalised

'Necessity participation' is a term to describe how citizen activism is provoked by urgent situations: when the lives of the people involved are at risk unless they take action, that is, participate in civic life. In the case of PLHA, the diagnosis was often a crucial moment that changed the way that people look at their lives and their political action. Activism and civic participation became urgently necessary to demand the services and rights from the state that PLHA needed. One participant said; 'here the state made the issue invisible, and we, the activists, had to pay for that. It was like paying something to make the problem of HIV/AIDS visible, but using your face. Many of us had to appear in the media, although nobody would have liked to have their diagnosis made public.'[xxv] Besides this, urgent participation creates 'necessity identities', that people's activism for the causes they are involved in begin to be part of their self conception.

However, citizens' practices change over time. Once the immediate urgency is addressed, the levels of participation may decline. Developing either a long-term agenda or political identities beyond immediate concerns seems to be less common. In this case, as in other countries, activism started to decline in Peru once free anti-retroviral treatment became available in 2004.

'Micro-participation' leading to citizen activism

According to activists' stories, a common turning point after the diagnosis was joining a mutual support group. These spaces allowed PLHA to have a very personal experience, sharing concerns, fears, experiences and problems in a group of peers, providing an alternative to the typical power dynamics of the individualising medical approach.

This personal level is very much linked to citizen action at the higher level of engaging with government to demand better rights. Personal and immediate experiences, which can be described as 'micro-participation', impact people's participation and involvement at the 'macro' political or institutional levels.

This personal level of micro participation was seen by some PHLA as the basis for other types of participation. One said: 'How do you create an activist? First, as there were no medicines nor anything that could save you, people with HIV started to create mutual support groups and that helped. With time, some people decided to change, and stopped just hugging each other and started to demand rights'.[xxvi]

So the personal dimensions of politics in HIV/AIDS activism are extremely important, and inseparable from the more traditional forms of citizen action for civil rights. Mutual support groups are an example of the personal becoming political, as personal support associations encourage a process of political awareness that forms the basis for explicitly activist groups and platforms. What Cornwall and Gaventa term 'created or claimed' participatory spaces like mutual support groups are crucial for improving a model like CONAMUSA, which is around 'invited' participatory spaces, where ministries do the inviting and NGOs and communities of PLHA do the participating.[xxvii]

Development practitioners and supporting activism

The difficult question for outside agencies trying to fund HIV/AIDS activism, such as the Global Fund, is how they can support already existing, vibrant and valuable initiatives such as mutual support groups without undermining the dedicated grassroots nature of the groups that makes them powerful. The concepts of 'necessity participation' and 'micro-participation' may be helpful to understand that strong citizen activism cannot be artificially created, but must be rooted in existing spaces and associations of citizens who have strong personal connections and a sense of urgency to address the state's deficiencies in providing them their own rights. The challenge here is that there may well be a need for external assistance, but it must be made appropriate to the group in question rather than being driven by external perceptions of what is needed and when.

Lessons

'Invited spaces' of political participation established by donors have limited impact. Instead, the 'created or claimed' spaces of people living with HIV/AIDS gathering in mutual support groups have been much more effective in giving birth to activism and engagement with civil rights. Supporters of HIV/AIDS activism should realise that these alternative spaces and networks that have been 'created or claimed' by the marginalised may be stronger and more participatory bases to work from than their own 'invited' spaces, such as the Global Fund's national 'Country Coordinating Mechanism' model. Grassroots groups' democratic practices provide a real base for promoting citizenship that is based on the rights of individuals and expressed collectively, but these groups are often overlooked. To overcome this, the following reforms of methodology are required:

- The strategy for activism needs to rely on dedicated and personal associations, such as mutual support groups.

- These groups should also feature in international standards, like the GIPA Principle for greater involvement of people living with HIV/AIDS.[18]

- The development of longer-term agendas should also be emphasised.

- In order to develop adequate participatory models, the participation of PLHA has to be understood in all its contradictions and dilemmas, particularly the fact that the issue is intensely private and personal, but must also become public and political if a positive change can be made.

Many of the lessons from this case will also be relevant in thinking about supporting civic activism for other marginalised groups in different contexts and how to adapt funding to such specific needs taking into account the strengths and weaknesses of the concerned social groups and associations.

---

[18] UNAIDS published the first guidelines for GIPA in 1999.

6.3 Programming for 'strong publics' in Central America

This case explores two long-term Irish Aid-funded projects on 'active citizenship', undertaken with regional universities in El Salvador, Nicaragua and Honduras. The overall aim of both projects was to build 'strong publics' of citizens capable of conceiving and voicing radical development alternatives.[19] One project tried to strengthen pro-poor research and advocacy and accompanying networks in civil society, and another tried to build civil society's capacity to influence pro-poor policy. Some spaces for discussion and networking were created but these were limited by gaps in understanding and the different purposes of distinct sections of civil society, which were difficult to overcome. Creating civil society networks with the capacities to work regionally to press governments to honour the collective social, economic and cultural rights of citizens is still a task in hand.

The first project tried to build more effective networks, on both a national and regional basis, for CSOs doing research and advocacy on pro-poor policy. Themes for research and advocacy included; women migrant social networks in Central America, the social and employment integration of people with disabilities in Nicaragua, and the impact of international aid over a decade in Honduras. Research was conducted on eight interesting themes across the three countries, but the networks remained weak and did not bring about the hoped-for regional perspective. Advocacy suffered as the participants were ultimately more interested in the research funds than advocacy activities. They saw themselves more as recipients than partners.

The second project involved capacity building, which aimed to strengthen policy influence on poverty issues through joint civil society–local government partnerships. The project funded scholarships for both NGO and local government staff to do Management Diplomas, and also tried to encourage the formation of joint research proposals from civil society and local government. The training for this was delivered by consultants, but the host universities were not happy. They felt that the content should relate more closely to NGO experience and balance the technical content, which was essentially a business and administration model, with an emphasis on geopolitical context and theory of development and civil society.

The expectation was that the programme's focus on research, advocacy and capacity building would contribute to 'strong publics'. This would mean civil society would be more active and effective as opinion formers, decision makers and contributors of alternative proposals on crucial contemporary issues – such as the impact of global recession, the failings of the neoliberal model and the prospects for the Central American Free Trade Agreement with the Obama Presidency.

Where the sweeping aim to support a sector challenging liberalising governments to honour their citizens' social, economic and cultural rights is laudable, the generalised approach made a 'strong public' challenging to achieve when different sectors of civil society have different priorities. The initiative did manage to create some spaces for regional discussion and networking, and research institutions gladly participated in research into pro-

---

[19] www.ciudadania-activa-ca.net

poor policies. However, they did not necessarily throw themselves into advocacy, and NGOs and local government partnerships were tense due to different perspectives, either technical or political. Programming focussed on think-tanks and universities, which inhabit very different parts of civil society from its more activist forms. Thus effective ways to support engagement between policy makers and the wider public – especially poor citizens who seek spaces for participation – remains elusive.

Lessons
Many Central American countries yearn for 'strong publics' that can incubate and nourish progressive visions through self-managed, opinion forming and decision making civic institutions. As with the case in Paraguay in Chapter 2 (see page 28) the lesson here is that externally-designed programmes for strengthening civil society often contain technically good elements but are too ambitious. They tend to assume that links between various segments of society can be easily engineered through programme work. More often, as in the Active Citizenship initiative in Paraguay, CSOs will come together for the benefits the programme offers, and carry out worthwhile activities, without developing sustainable networks that last beyond funding.

Civil society is multi faceted, made up of a diverse range of actors with different primary interests. To support CSOs as 'makers and shapers' of civic spaces, civil society programmes need to be designed and executed with a careful contextual understanding of the characteristics, capacities, aims and visions of different parts of society. Without this, it will be difficult to gain the full commitment of local actors and to build effective networks that allow them to play complementary roles. Even then, programmes such as this can support the enabling environment for citizen action but they cannot create strong publics, the foundation of which has to be autonomous, self-organised citizens' associations or movements.

6.4 Ethnic associations confront the state in Amazonia[xxviii]

With 60,000 members, the Awajún are one of the four biggest ethnic groups of the Peruvian Amazon. Over the last 30 years they, and the rest of the indigenous people of the lowlands, have built strong representative structures at community level and extended them to the capital. In 1980 they founded AIDESEP, an ethnic association to represent the poorest and most marginalised peoples of Peru. Their needs were many but the fundamental work of the organisation was always to secure territorial rights over their lands and defend them against newcomers. For the indigenous peoples it was a question of survival – they knew all too well the devastation that the extractive industries caused to their forests and their people's health.

AIDESEP gradually strengthened its capacity to represent its communities, earning a degree of respect and legitimacy with successive governments. The progressive realisation of the indigenous people's rights to their territory was interrupted with the election of Alan Garcia in 2006. Garcia had been a populist anti-American President of Peru who bankrupted the country in the mid-1980s and was driven into exile. 15 years later he returned as a neoliberal and immediately put in motion a fire-sale of the country's considerable hydrocarbon and mineral assets. AIDESEP, along with other indigenous social movements, challenged the legality of the sale, on the grounds that their right to free and informed prior consultation and consent had been violated.

The Awajún applied pressure by closing down all road and river traffic in the northern forest. Over several months from early 2009 the government failed to negotiate, and then only in bad faith. The President inflamed the strikers by accusing them of a 'dog in the manger' attitude. What he meant was that they were selfishly unwilling to sacrifice their environment for the good of the country, but the people understood he was literally calling Indians 'dogs', which became obvious to them when he went on to say they were 'second class citizens'.

Even so AIDESEP decided to negotiate. But while the Awajún were dismantling their barricades, the government ordered anti-terrorist police to take control of the jungle town of Bagua. The ensuing violence caused 40 deaths and hundreds of wounded. In retaliation the government clamped down on the indigenous movement. It tried to arrest the leadership of AIDESEP but Nicaragua offered political asylum. The government then pursued AIDESEP as a terrorist organisation, but the highest court in Peru expressed doubts that there was a case. Eventually the government was forced back to the negotiating table.

In defence of their legal rights, the Awajún and AIDESEP however were drawn inexorably deeper into 'big P' politics. A long-term campaign that started with the 'small p' demand for the right of consultation over the use of their territory escalated into a full scale attack on the government's record. For its part the ruling APRA had canvassed on a manifesto of defiance against multi-national capital but once in office had run riot over the constitution to rush through a free trade agreement with the United States.

Lessons

Claiming citizenship requires engagement between state and society, and an acceptance of the rights of citizen by the state. Both must engage with one another within the law to avoid conflict. Civil society provides the means of claiming citizenship rights by continuously airing issues of governance as they arise through the political process. The obligation of citizens is to be constantly vigilant in the interests of a healthy society. The corresponding obligation of the executive is to respond, engaging its ministers and officials in the ongoing debate, thereby acknowledging in daily practice that the government of the day derives its legitimacy from the quality of justification it provides for its actions. Once the state disengages itself from the debate, or unilaterally sets the terms of discussion, or manoeuvres to suppress key individuals and institutions of civil society, then the state no longer commands legitimacy. The reason why it is so essential to support civil society to fulfil all its five functions is that once the potential for citizens to promote their rights through civil society is lost, 'uncivil society' and its violent means may be the only methods left to contest the state's authority. The previous case from the indigenous movement of lowland Peru is a reflection of just such a situation.

Recommendations

The cases in this chapter show that supporting a strong sense of citizenship and citizen rights is an area that is difficult to engineer through external programming. The need for contextual understanding is as important here as in other chapters. Nonetheless, there are several key strategic ideas that we recommend practitioners take on board when aiming to support civil society's capacity to strengthen citizenship.

1. Keep the 'right to have rights' alive
Civic, even constitutional gains under one regime can be quickly lost under another. The cautionary lesson from partially democratic regions like Central America is that civil society needs to be constantly on guard against authoritarian tendencies in government, whether from the left or the right. It has also been argued that similar slippage has occurred in Africa where in newly independent states civil society felt it should or could not criticise the government, their liberators from colonial rule. When authoritarianism and corruption finally become too obvious to ignore then it is often too late – Zimbabwe is a painful example of this.

Brazil, in contrast, buried its authoritarian past with the concept of 'social citizenship'. The case of Sao Paulo's homeless citizens' movement (see Chapter 4, page 55) demonstrates that anything less than the full implementation of civic rights diminishes citizenship in Brazil and impoverishes the quality of society as a whole. Social movements derive legitimacy from protesting the violation of rights guaranteed by the constitution and insisting that the state addresses them. For civil society to claim citizenship, the engagement of the state as guarantor of citizenship rights is required too. Donors can ensure that they work towards an enabling environment, and support people's movements who call for constitutional rights and laws to be honoured.

2. Call for rights but also support citizens to take responsibility as 'makers and shapers'
Citizens' ability to take responsibility and realise their rights are important building blocks to a more democratic system. It is essential that programmes recognise both sides of the equation. Talking rights is a good start, but the responsibilities of engaging with the formal political process, voting, running for office, must also be supported. Civic education stresses these and should be a component of any attempt to support citizens to claim and enhance their rights.

Civil society at its best is the nursery for some of these basic skills, as CSOs have often been able to offer both the rights education as well as helping people understand and participate in their responsibilities. As mentioned in other chapters, the telling factor as to whether a CSO will be effective in supporting civil rights and responsibilities is if there are participatory process and structures in place. It is not enough to talk about citizens' rights if the institution promoting them is a closed, top down organisation.

Participation as a citizen may take many different forms depending on the power relationships, the context, culture and history of a people. But we do need to ensure that programmes supporting 'citizen participation' do not just promote the participation of a minority or an elite. Furthermore, involvement in grassroots participation should lead to and go hand in hand with participation in wider societal processes. Thus civil society should lead by example and seek ways of helping socially excluded groups enter the wider polity, whether through basic education and training, removing constraints on their participation, or ensuring that the state works within the rule of the law. A helpful litmus test of how equitable 'participation' is, is to ask whether citizens are proactive 'makers and shapers' of alternatives, able to achieve agency in citizenship – or are they merely passive 'users and choosers' of pre-ordained programmes or services.[xxix]

3. Protect and enhance rights of association

The right of association has to be one of the key elements of supporting the rights and concept of citizenship, because it underlines the whole concept of collective action by citizens. It is essential that citizens can meet together for a myriad of reasons; whether it is for self help, managing a local school, discussing issues of common concern, lobbying local government, defending a perceived injustice against them, complaining about a government action and so on. The ability to meet and organise is a backbone of civil society. Many organisations have recognised this and have taken steps through political and legal channels as well as the media to protect and enhance the right of association.

The cases illustrate that citizens, especially the marginalised, value associations. It is a distortion in most if not all contexts to argue that associations of civil society are no longer relevant in an age of 'unscripted civic action' by individuals.[xxx] The claim is that citizens can come together when the need presents itself. However, we need to be aware that this 'unscripted civic action' is an analysis that can favour elites that already have well developed networks. Thus our emphasis here is on permitting all members of society the option of organising as they feel appropriate and in the manner they choose – and therefore external resources are sometimes necessary to avoid associational life being dominated by those with their own resources.

4. Support legal aid which enhances individual and collective equality

A drive for equality by citizens, as individuals, but often for a broad group of individuals marginalised for the same reason, is another key principle that many practitioners organise around. Legal aid to individuals is well established in many countries. The most successful programmes use the individual case to force recognition of general rules and legal precedents, hence achieving a wider impact. A strategic approach to legal aid can have an important multiplier effect. The concept of the rule of law is one which has been established through long struggle by civil societies in many countries. Many civil society groups have implicitly worked towards achieving this principle for its members and others. The focus on minorities and others treated prejudicially by the state or even other groups has been common amongst NGOs and other CSOs.

However, it is important to remember that although people can co-opt the language of government (laws, rights, constitution), equally government can co-opt the language of civil society and the citizen. Hence civic values such as equality of opportunity, participation, empowerment, voice and governance frequently crop up in political rhetoric as camouflage for less than progressive approaches. The widespread abuse of the term 'participation' which came to be used during the days of structural adjustment as a euphemism for cost-recovery is an example. At worst, attempts by the state to 'run' civil society must be recognised for what they are, as attempts to ensure authoritarian control and deny real rights of the citizen.

Summary of key points

Successful states need to guarantee the rights of citizens, and support active citizenship in an independent civil society which is free to generate ideas and actions for the public good. In turn, vibrant civil societies need tolerant governments to guarantee civil society's democratic rights.

However, many governments try to occupy the civic space, pushing out any dissident voices and monopolising public debate, rather than supporting active citizenship. Civil society in these contexts will need to actively defend its rights to participate in politics and to shape policy.

'Created or claimed' spaces of association, such as mutual support groups for those living with HIV/AIDS, may provide stronger bases for supporting citizen activism of the marginalised than 'invited' spaces created by INGOs or officials. Support for citizenship has to rely on these groups of 'makers and shapers' of citizenship.

'Strong publics' cannot be created from the outside, although civil society programmes can help support elements of an enabling environment. This can mean ensuring that the right of association is protected, and attempting to enhance it by building civil society networks.

Those seeking to support civil society's ability to promote citizenship should both talk about civil rights but also support the practice of civil responsibilities in terms of political engagement, and should understand the power of legal channels for enhancing collective equality.

7

How to support civil society over the next decade

Drawing on the cases explored in the previous chapters and INTRAC's years of experience with civil society, this chapter provides advice to development practitioners who wish to support civil society effectively. The chapter starts with an analysis of successful approaches to strengthening civil society and looks at how to build on these successes. It then summarises the continuing problems that have contributed to the current crisis in civil society support and suggests what we can do to reform them. Next, we put forward a number of key strategic recommendations for development practitioners. The chapter closes with a pointers directing civil society strengthening efforts towards the goal of an autonomous civil society.

7.1 What are the most promising approaches to take us forward?

Until recently, the message from research findings was that the growth of CSOs has been so great that it amounted to an 'associational revolution', and that this 'revolution' was led by NGOs. Yet NGOs are only a small minority in comparison to the vast volume of associational life that often goes unnoticed: for the most part, informal organisations of every kind of membership, each with a cause or mission to uphold.

Expectations are growing that these civic associations will demand that governments across the globe change beyond recognition: opening up to citizen participation far beyond an inclusion of traditional ruling cliques and radically improving their performance. NGOs need to ask themselves how they can best support this social phenomenon, putting their experience at the disposal of a diverse range of civil society actors of all different shapes and sizes. They must acknowledge where, for self interest, they have hindered the autonomy and capacity of these organisations, and modify their policy and practice accordingly. Donors also bear a heavy responsibility to make sure that their resources are in the right place and appropriately accessible when they are needed. So where have there been promising approaches to working with civil society, and how best can we build upon them?

Building on civil society strengths

What has gone right?	How to build on successes
A more prominent role for civil society in development.	Develop expertise to **identify and support those** progressive elements of civil society 'beyond NGOs', **which have firm roots** in the population.[1]
Inspirational examples of CSOs confronting political and social injustices.	Support diverse civil society groups working for more just societies. **Define your role in supporting civil society** – which functions to prioritise, where, why and how? Work should build on best practices developed in partnership approaches.
Private sector, state and multilateral actors increasingly engage with civil society actors.	**Safeguard** civil society **autonomy and diversity** as the basis of civil society's growing power, whilst **developing coordinated approaches to take on strategic challenges** that can make a real impact on social justice.
The spread of advocacy as a tool for social justice.	Ensure advocacy **reflects the voices of grassroots experience**, and is **embedded in empowering processes** which build the capacities of those involved.
A conceptual shift from needs-based to rights-based approaches.	Maintain a rights-based focus, and **support grassroots movements, particularly those with strong membership bases, that are using the language of rights** to call for change, as well as CBOs and NGOs.
A focus on strengthening capacities at all levels of civil society.	**Maintain focus on capacity building that is holistic and serves CSOs' sovereignty**. This should go along with **supporting an enabling environment** for future capacitated' partners to be able to work well.

The size and scope of civil society has been described as a 'global associational revolution'[1].[xxxi] Whilst much effective civic association pre-exists, or exists beyond the growth of NGOs, this label does reflect a growing sense of **positive expectations and rising support for civil society**. Overall, this embracing of activism and voluntary commitment is a major achievement of modern societies. It has become clear that civil society institutions enjoy greater public trust and support than political parties in many different contexts – even in well-established democracies. However, we need to keep in mind that not all growth is necessarily positive, and may even be counter productive to a strong civil society. We need to look beyond the growth of organisations that are emerging through contract-culture funding.

By building local NGOs in their own image, official aid and large northern INGOs active in the South risk creating an artificial society that is highly dependent upon external presence and resources. Instead, development practitioners should seek a deeper understanding

---

[1] See box on 'Understanding civil society in your own context' on page 106.

of what it means for civil society movements, associations and organisations to be rooted in their own societies, and to support other manifestations of vibrant civil society such as social movements and networks. Otherwise in the South the rhetoric of 'civil society' will be seen as just another northern fad – ignored at best, or at worst harnessed to the ends of the privileged.

The revival of understanding civil society as a political space and force – rather than just a means of voluntary service provision – has stimulated self-organised citizen participation at a time of lacklustre political life.[xxxii] Inspiring examples discussed in this book include southern alliances campaigning against enforced disappearances, advocacy journalism tackling human rights abuse, social movements making good use of civic rights enshrined in constitutions – and protecting them when governments renege on commitments. Donors, governments, and INGOs have also shown some degree of **recognition of civil society as a political actor**. However, while it is true that a renewed interest in civil society has galvanised promising statements about the nature and role of civil society at the level of policy, there is a danger of slippage. There is a question as to why, despite good policies regarding civil society, many organisations often fall short in practice. Why do some organisations find it difficult to achieve objectives to support civil society? Is it the negative impact of other demands on the aid industry, including institutional self-interest, which divert good intentions? Partnership approaches have been squeezed out by the aid industry pressures, and once partnership is lost, the main tool for strengthening civil society disappears. All work with civil society should build on best practices developed in INGO partnership work. Alongside this partnership ethos, the main way that INGOs can practically support civil society is to be much clearer about their roles. Thinking about the functions of civil society as outlined in this book is a useful starting point. INGOs should ask themselves 'which function(s) should we be supporting in which contexts?' and 'how can we best support civil society to fulfil these functions?'.

The increasing recognition of civil society means that the private sector, the state and multilateral development agencies regularly express a need for **inclusion and engagement with civil society's 'voice'**. Civil society has earned this recognition in development policy through persisting with a principled stand, pressuring the powerful for major shifts such as the eventual abandonment of structural adjustment. Civil society is now recognised as a distinct 'voice' to be consulted, to participate, and to have an influence. The challenge for the future is to ensure civil society can find a common voice and use this new-found influence strategically at the international level, without compromising its autonomy and diversity. This will require far more debate and cooperation between civil society groups and with other actors at all levels to build understanding and expertise of how best to exert influence. Strengthening networks and the relational capacity of civil society should be a priority, while bearing in mind that civil society's autonomy from market and state is its most precious asset – this should be safeguarded and build upon for its voice to have critical value. Civil society's diversity must also be protected, by respecting the distinct purposes of the organisations that coordinate with one another.

There is much **wider use of advocacy to achieve social justice**, and greater recognition of the value of advocacy in development at all levels: local, regional, national, and international. We know that strong civil societies are capable of requiring states to organise to meet citizens' individual and collective rights. CSOs need to insist that international cooperation of all forms should be directed to advocacy based in participatory and equal processes, and not to just to continually alleviate needs through international humanitarian and operational work. As a caveat to this strength, as many of our examples showed, there is a need to build upon the emerging realisation that service provision and advocacy are two ends of a spectrum that should enhance and inform one another. It should also be noted that local civil society actors can feel displaced and devalued by global campaigns 'parachuted' into their society, and people can feel alienated and intimidated by highly politicised NGOs. INGOs must develop clearer views of which type of advocacy is appropriate in different circumstances, and what the roles of different actors are. Global players must be much more accountable to local civil society actors, who should determine their own advocacy agenda. Advocacy that is rooted in local level practical work and owned by indigenous associations will be more powerful, genuine, and of long-term benefit to strengthening the capacities of independent national civil actors.[xxxiii] To serve this, the aid industry must regain their innovatory zeal for participation, especially in approaches that involve power analysis, and continually seek out opportunities to advocate for enhanced citizen voice in pro-poor policies, which may otherwise end up as top-down redistribution efforts.

The shift from needs-based to rights-based approaches is a very important development for civil society. Potentially, it may provide an internationally understood language that can be used by grassroots organisations of the marginalised to call for change. As several of the case studies have demonstrated, the rights-based approach has been particularly important for membership-based groups to maintain a long-term focus on bringing about positive changes in the lives of their constituencies. There is a need to protect this long-term vision from the pressures of civil society initiatives funded by the contract culture, where the focus is short-term, target-driven efficiency. More emphasis should be placed on enhancing membership-based groups' effectiveness in supporting different constituencies to realise their civil, political, economic, social or cultural rights. Local actors should also decide on the prioritisation of rights. NGOs can build on their experience of shifting to rights-based approaches to assess the effectiveness of different ways of helping others do so. All too often the shift is in language alone. As some of the cases show, there is room to innovate around NGOs' roles to support the 'right to have rights' of severely marginalised but organised population groups, and to take a role in supporting southern networks of these groups.

Strengthening the capacities of local actors at all levels in civil society is the key to long-term success. The development community has greatly improved its understanding of capacity-building processes and the skills and understanding exist to engage in constructive mutual partnerships with local development actors. The strength should not be undercut by a realisation that 'capacity building' has at worst been a falsely hyped 'magic bullet'. Overall, the focus on capacity building has made it possible for extensive experimentation on what it takes to help individual, organisational and institutional civic actors strengthen their societies. It is essential that this focus is maintained, even if it becomes evident that stronger civil societies may have a negative impact on the growth prospects of some development cooperation agencies. The fact that some capacity building has been used in an instrumental manner to mould organisations into the aid process highlights the need for ensuring that capacity building encompasses a long-term, holistic view.

By 'holistic capacities' we mean not just the CSO's performance in terms of outcomes and impact, but also its organisational health and, crucially, its ability to develop and maintain those relational capacities that are essential for deepening civil society. CSOs like these succeed when capacity development focuses on serving their 'intrinsic capacity' – their constituency's 'sovereign' purpose, often one that speaks directly to people's aspirations and rights. The strength of their capacities is derived from the energy of their members, and listening to them rather than 'professionalising' for the aid industry. The Community Development Resource Association (CDRA)[2], a South African CSO with a background in grassroots organisational development and a long-term commitment in bringing the 'periphery to the centre', discusses what makes 'sovereign CSOs' effective in the box below. Capacity building that serves these holistic purposes will better allow those involved to innovate around strategies for future cooperation and solidarity with their partners. An accompanying support for the enabling environment is also necessary to allow the capacities of civil society groupings to be exercised.

Example: Capacity building for sovereign CSOs

CDRA is an organisation which cares passionately about active, relevant, responsive and resilient local civil societies. They believe that when the objective is to strengthen social capital, or indeed any of the five functions of civil society, donors and INGO partners must be careful not to reduce civil society at the community level to contractors of top-down development models.

The functions of a flourishing civil society, such as producing trust, networks and reciprocity, can only be carried out effectively by sovereign organisations pursuing their own purposes, in their own way and with allies of their own choosing.

CDRA asks us to rephrase the development question from 'how do we make change happen?' to 'how do authentic local organisations and social movements emerge and develop?' By way of reply it defines a sovereign CSO as one that:

- Works with its own purpose and values
- Expresses the will and voice of its own constituents
- Is culturally and structurally unique, rather than a 'best practice' clone
- Is politically conscious and asks its own questions
- Is able to cooperate and collaborate
- Is able to learn and adapt from its own experience.

According to CDRA, those carrying out capacity building efforts should be thoughtful about how they do so. If the capacity building is limited to expertise in development techniques, such as managing the project cycle, the result may be assimilation to the aid industry, and an organisation being 'cloned' – implementing projects which are part of strategies designed by others.

Capacity building with local organisations should counteract this risk by focussing efforts on encouraging horizontal linkages with other CSOs. This can be more effective – and it builds networks that strengthen social capital.

---

[2] See www.cdra.org.za

7.2 Ways to address continuing challenges

If civil society strengthening as an end in itself is of paramount importance to sustainably tackle inequality and poverty, as this book has argued, there are some fundamental challenges for those working with civil society. Thinking in terms of the benefits of the five functions of civil society to citizens will call for a change in the way many agencies conceive of aid. NGOs and donors should not continue with 'business as usual' if this is focussed on short-term goals merely dealing with the symptoms of poverty. The major challenge seen throughout the book has been the loss of autonomy for some aspects of civil society due to the dominance of professionalised NGOs, whose approaches may dull an agenda driven by grassroots organisations. Such problems need to be acknowledged and acted upon.

Civil society organisations need to be supported as 'makers and shapers' of change, not 'users and choosers' of priorities driven by donors, national governments, or INGO partners.[xxxiv] INGOs bear a good part of the responsibility for changing this, and the table below summarises some key areas where we believe that reform is needed.

Ways of overcoming challenges in working with civil society

What has gone wrong?	What is to be done about it?
There has been a loss of autonomy for civil society, as agendas dealing with symptoms of poverty have supplanted support for local civil society.	Civil society strengthening must become more than a label for a high level of INGO activity. Concrete strategies to support civil society to fulfil its functions, contextual analysis, and a sector-wide approach should be prioritised.
NGOs more interested in protecting their institutional growth have reduced citizens to consumers, rather than supporting alternative ideas from autonomous, diverse civil society actors.	Even if it undermines their current ways of working and long-term survival, INGOs should embrace an approach that develops local organisations, funding potentially risky innovations. Progressive groups should reinstate the role of civil society in holding the state and market to account and as a site for alternatives.
The INGO culture of results-based management has displaced values-based leadership, weakening local accountability and legitimacy.	Restore partnership as the primary relationship between CSOs of the North and South. This means increasing local participation, finding new tools which take into account longer term impact, placing a high value on direct accountability to local actors, and addressing broader problems of professionalisation such as salary inflation and undermining voluntarism.

Civil society strengthening is a valid end in itself
Concrete strategies to support civil society to fulfil its broader functions, contextual analysis, and a sector-wide approach should be prioritised. One fundamental criticism of civil society is that – far from being a site of innovation and alternatives – it has been reduced to

a component of the aid industry, propping up tired mainstream solutions. This loss of autonomy has undermined civil society's political vocation and sanitised it to become an implementing mechanism for technical approaches to poverty reduction.[xxxv] The overarching agendas of the aid industry, such as the Millennium Development Goals, have supplanted a focus on the intrinsic value of civil society. Whilst the 'civil society-led' Open Forum on Aid Effectiveness aims to bring an understanding of civil society's perspective on development into the highest levels of the aid architecture, the jury remains out on how possible and desirable a concrete definition of 'effectiveness' is, and whether this can support civil society and guarantee its autonomy and diversity.

The well-intentioned funding of 'civil society' from official donors and INGOs can at times undermine or at least taint the integrity and independence of CSOs. When external resources are more important than support from members, attention shifts away from the constituency and towards the donor, creating an unhealthy climate of 'upward accountability; in other words, dependence. Donor interests can serve to maintain the global status quo rather than to attack the root causes of poverty and conflict, which are often injustice and discrimination. There is a need to recognise that many elements in civil society will also adopt the language of the donors for status and financial gain rather than due to conviction.

A much more vigorous and sustained effort is needed to identify, support and sustain civic initiatives that are trying to reform societies so that they function better over the long term.[xxxvi] Practitioners should recognise and support those local organisations with their own dedicated visions as the basis for change, rather than external agendas. The current donor distancing from sector-wide civil society support – the 'taming of civil society' – is at least partly due to civil society rediscovering its distinctive, alternative voice. Instead, sector-wide civil society support as an end worth funding in itself, and nuanced, context-sensitive support should become the hallmark of good donorship. Donors and NGOs need to be much more conscious about the risk of creating perverse incentives within civil society. Flooding particular civil societies with resources not available in the state or market sectors is counter-productive, as it drains these sectors of capacity and incites envy. Instead, INGO poverty programmes should be supportive of longer term capacity building of local civil society and link meeting needs to 'small p' political engagement. Furthermore, there should be more South–South exchange of experience rather than the traditional North–South distribution of resources and agendas. Both northern and southern NGOs must resist the need to grow at the expense of their missions.

INGOs should embrace an approach that develops local organisations, funding potentially risky innovations

A number of criticisms centre around the perception that citizens are reduced to consumers of solutions produced by professionalised NGOs, more interested in their own institutional growth and survival than in supporting civil society 'alternatives'. There is a persistent belief in some progressive circles that the rhetoric of 'civil society' is just the latest label in an agenda to further neo-liberalism. Indeed, the concept of civil society does assume certain freedoms to individuals and groups of individuals in relation to an overbearing state. On the other hand, it also encompasses traditional forms of association, which work for collective rights. Civil society can accommodate most political perspectives, apart from those which preclude any form of non-state actor.

However, there is some merit in the critics' caution. The imperative towards institutional growth of many professionalised INGOs seems to trump values-bases. In many societies of the former Soviet Union, western NGOs are seen as a crusading instrument of extreme forms of free market capitalism under a system of 'turbo-capitalism', where citizens are reduced to passive consumers, exercising choice over products not governance.[xxxvii] Within the INGO world there is a debate as to how to maintain values of partnering with local civil societies with the imperative to meet the current demands of globalised aid. Many organisations are struggling to find this balance and this debate needs to continue. Progressive groups need to be clear about their agendas to reinstate the role of citizens and civil society as key elements in holding the state and market to account through a multitude of ways – elections, budget monitoring, complaints mechanisms – and as a site for alternatives to systems that are failing. Progressive civil society itself needs to make civic activism more relevant, compelling, cutting-edge and effective.

All work with civil society must be grounded in accountability to the constituency

Civil society has become unduly dominated by NGOs which have often shifted 'from membership to management', becoming professional at the expense of real commitment.[xxxviii] NGOs have monopolised large parts of both civic space and the development agenda at the expense of other actors. Whilst professionalisation is not necessarily negative, it is important to look for emerging and diverse forms and actors in civil society, which may generate more energy than organisations focussed on their own professionalism. The cases in this book show some good examples of work with civil society emanating from large INGOs in partnership with CSOs. But we also need to take a longer-term perspective beyond NGOs, that more can be achieved by organisations that have dedicated members and purposes that stretch beyond one-to-three-year funding cycles. To work effectively with such organisations, donors and INGOs need new tools which take into account longer-term impact beyond tangible outputs.

INGOs must encourage membership organisations to come forward and directly express their opinions and expectations, and work with their agendas rather than external global corporate goals. We need to place NGOs within a more realistic and subservient position as regards other associations when drawing up a civil society strengthening strategy in a particular context. Donors must encourage other groups that may not necessarily see themselves as belonging in 'civil society', such as social movements, cultural associations, chambers of commerce, burial societies, cooperatives, trade unions, professional associations and so on. Furthermore, a more even-handed approach by donors can encourage civil society without merely instrumentalising it, and therefore sidelining its important socio-political roles. However, these problems extend beyond INGOs to many local NGOs who, in embracing funding from the aid industry, have inherited many of the problems afflicting INGOs. These include a loss of autonomy in relation to the government, lack of accountability to those on whose behalf they work, and the contract-driven demands of professionalisation. Importantly, these segments of local civil society may undermine the volunteerism and membership basis that characterises the sort of civil society we have held up as having the potential to really enact substantial change.

There is a better understanding of working to strengthen southern CSOs – and it is genuine partnership. Partnership in its original sense implies mutual rights and obligations within equal relationships between CSOs in both the North and the South. Extended further, such partnerships can benefit innovative south–south collaborations, which democratise the aid industry in exciting new ways, for example with the 'movement for the disappeared' (see Chapter 3, page 39). The huge positive here is that the attitudes and skills for strengthening civil society gained at the cutting edge over two decades of aid are sustained.

7.3 What can practitioners do?

Previous chapters finished with recommendations that emerged in the light of the cases. Here we make some more general recommendations, based on good practice and clear strategic directions that have emerged from these case studies and INTRAC's many years of work with civil society:

a. Understand civil society in the contexts you work
b. Help build an environment that enables civil society to achieve its functions
c. Promote a balanced approach to development
d. Go beyond individual CSOs or projects
e. Be innovative about funding
f. Focus on longer term impact
g. Quality not quantity
h. Build capacity at multiple levels
i. Nurture civil society in countries that 'graduate' from aid

a. Understand civil society in the contexts you work

There are many useful ways outsiders can support local civil society, but these always require thought and contextualisation. To support civil society as an end in itself, or at least not to weaken or pervert it, it is important to see how civil society fits with the wider society and polity. There is a growing realisation of that contextual understanding of politics and culture is essential, especially in terms of gaining insights into power relations within a society that could greatly affect work with civil society. The questions in the box below can be used as a toolkit to give the basic background to civil society in the context you are working. Regular reviews of context and programme should be undertaken. Appendix 3 provides a very detailed example of mapping CSOs in Ethiopia.

> **Understanding civil society in your own context**
> - Is civil society inclusive of all aspects of society (or only serving one group or gender for example), or is it dominated by an elite?
> - How much does it allow for both horizontal and vertical linkages (alliances between groups, contacts with others such as the government or international bodies)?
> - How thick or thin is local civil society – are citizens members of more than one group, or are they determined by a single membership (e.g. ethnic, village, professional)? How many overlapping memberships can we identify which have a meaning for people? Do these dilute the single-focus nature of some social labels – can they create broader allegiances and build tolerance?
> - Are there representative bodies of different aspects of civil society (e.g. networks, chambers of commerce, professional associations, trade unions)?
> - How coherent is the legal framework for civil society? Does the rule of law really apply to relations between the state and civil society?
> - Is there something to be said about the sequencing of civil society functions in different governance situations – through, for example, identifying whether one function or another is more suitable in emerging democracies than in authoritarian states?

In very vulnerable situations with antagonistic governments, it may be a case of identifying what is possible, and funding even limited actions in order to keep the space for civil society open, rather than be overly ambitious. There are good historical cases of this, for example; funding church-backed groups under Pinochet in Chile in the 1970s and 80s built the basis for the rapid re-emergence of civil society when the dictatorship finally came to an end. In such circumstances donors would do well not to necessarily take a project at face value, but to step back and consider the wider view of whether it will help maintain the capacities of civil society and provide the basis for it to develop faster once this becomes possible. Frequent smaller grants might be helpful in situations of local uncertainty to help groups be responsive as required. In dire circumstances, it is important to offer concrete services not just 'empowerment', but even then there must be a conscious policy and programme to ensure that the short-term delivery is done in such a way as to contribute to longer-term development rather than just immediate relief.

b. Help build an environment that enables civil society to achieve its functions

We have seen countless attempts by governments to constrain civil society, oppress populations and rule for their own benefit. The external world has a clear role in supporting the enabling environment for civil society, as well as other aspects of society and the market. One major bilateral donor's guidelines on civil society calls on its embassies to act to defend civil society and its roles.[xxxix] In other words, regardless of whether it had an aid programme and whether or not that included a civil society component, it was considered to be important for this country to argue for a strong independent civil society. Such a policy rightly recognises the value of civil society as an end in itself in terms of the benefits the five functions of civil society deliver to citizens. To strengthen the enabling environment there are technical issues around registration, taxation, and legal status, which international organisations can help their local partners with through sharing different models, legal frameworks, and good practice.

c. Promote a balanced approach to development

The continuing trend for NGOs to work purely as service deliverers has diverted attention away from the genuine building of the autonomous and longer-term capacity of local civil society. The concept of civil society as a source of cheap labour to fulfil certain service delivery targets is not unique to the developing world, but in resource-poor environments this approach can cause as much damage as good. We have also argued that an 'advocacy only' approach to supporting civil society is a correcting shift that has often been taken too far. Advocacy and service delivery are two, mutually strengthening, sides of the same coin – there is no point in promoting a policy reform that is not implemented in practice. Whilst the greater emphasis on advocacy is praiseworthy, where service delivery is bottom-up and linked to members' movements that try to influence those in power, it can be very much part of the five functions of civil society.

Similarly we need to recognise that many local NGOs have recreated the model whereby communities become dependent on externally driven inputs. As we can see in those countries where for various reasons donors leave – usually due to their attainment of middle-income status – what matters is that local civil society, rather than a group of salaried NGO workers, survives the end of aid. Thus NGOs must focus far more on preparing poor communities to cope after aid, through developing their capacities to advocate independently or to organise sustainable options for the future, for example based on their own voluntary activities, membership fees or local fundraising. INGOs' balanced interventions should prepare their partners to survive after donors leave, focussing on helping to strengthen community organisations that can stand unaided.

Balance is also sorely needed in attitudes towards the role of the state in development. The mainstream attitude has veered wildly over the last 30 years, from central to marginal. Each swing is accompanied by armies of aid industry consultants engaged to implement standardised policies across the developing world. Civil society is inevitably caught up in the process for as the state is 'rolled back', civil society is 'rolled forward' to exercise broad governance roles as well as to pick up any erstwhile state functions that are unattractive to the private sector, such as health or education for the poor. When it is the turn of the state to be emphasised again, officials are free to put NGOs back in their place. So the solution is clearly in favour of longer-term balanced approaches to development – wherever there is still the opportunity to work to a longer-term strategy.

d. Go beyond individual CSOs or projects

One constant aim is to get communities and CSOs to take responsibility for their own development rather than merely artificially creating organisations with minimal chance of surviving in the future. In other words, NGOs and donors active in the South must act in a way which strengthens civil society as a whole, beyond specific projects or specific organisations. Donors can have a great impact by taking a sector-wide approach, encouraging cooperation and coordination within civil society and between it and the state and market sectors, or via the media to the public at large. Operationally, this might lead to a mixed bag of grants rather than a focus on one sector (e.g. water, microcredit) which is the tendency of many donors. Similarly, an explicit focus on civil society diversity might lead to a portfolio including a think tank, a peasant union, legal aid, a radio programme, a volunteering centre, a council of indigenous groups, and so on. Donors and INGOs need to think through the funding mechanisms appropriate for reaching diverse CSOs across different sectors, and building the relational capacity and networks in the society overall.

e. Be innovative about funding

There is a need for responsive and sometimes independent donors who can act to respond to the urgent requirements of civil societies. There are already some such donors with a focus on specific issues or groups such as those helping indigenous groups or women leaders with legal support. Such support can go a long way in providing funding at the right scale and often has a significant impact on structural constraints on civil society. The move to create local foundations should take into account not just repeating other forms of financial support to local civil society, but looking towards those areas most requiring support to ensure a health civil society. For example, it has been suggested that the creation of a special funding mechanism, possibly hosted within the UN, might be able to support civil society independent of governments and short-term donor fashions. This would give a predictable source of support to CSOs regardless of the economic status of their home country or constraints they face from governments that are not supportive of civil society.

f. Focus on longer-term impact

A genuine focus on impact would also help to creat an improved learning loop to inform programme design and decision making, which would lead to better civil society support. Unfortunately, this is sorely missing in too much development aid. At the moment too much of the aid industry is wedded to short-term targets, and a focus on outputs rather than genuinely striving towards development impact. The managerialism behind the target culture may be acceptable in manufacturing, but it is inappropriate for changing societies, attitudes, educating individuals and developing institutions. Some donors have been able to sponsor serious analysis of societies and countries with a view to identifying where they can best contribute in light of local needs, culture, existing priorities and resources. However, many others lurch from one idea and project to another with little strategy, contextualisation of approach or thought as to the real impact of their efforts. Donors need to work out long-term development strategies with all stakeholders in the countries they support, and stick with the strategy long enough to give it a chance of making a difference. This would send a positive message to those groups seeking to work for and measure longer-term change in the lives of individuals, institutions and societies with which they are working.

g. Quality not quantity

The present obsession with scale and reduced transaction costs can be counter-productive in the context of civil society. Civil society success should not be equated with large-scale projects or large institutions.[3] Instead, small-scale experimental funding that takes risks in order to support innovation can have a high impact. Programmes which take a more strategic longe- term view may well end up spending quite small amounts of money but have far greater influence in the long term. A relatively modest sum can open doors, develop sectors, support new ideas, and keep spaces open for debate, independent research and advocacy, This in turn can develop responses to the state on issues of concern to special groups, such as the disabled, war veterans, victims of domestic violence, water users, and so on.

Rushing in with large programmes does not necessarily develop local civil society. Bilateral civil society strengthening programmes are often too ambitious, offering the earth in unrealistic time scales. These bilateral programmes should not try to do the job of local actors – former bishop Lugo won the election that gave democracy a chance in Paraguay, not USAID (see Chapter 2, page 28), although there was a role for external funding and for civil society support in Paraguay at a realistic and appropriate level.

h. Build capacity at multiple levels

The recognition of civil society's intrinsic value should also direct us to attempts to build up the depth of civil society, create strong linkages between different sections of it, and confront some of the legal and other constraints on civil society, such as fragmentation and the tendency to compete rather than cooperate. This should lead to interventions at different levels. The table below sets out a range of common support interventions at different levels of civil society. The focus on capacity building can be at one or multiple levels, but in all cases there needs to be a good understanding of the effects of intervention at one level upon the other levels – the main idea being to promote linkages between them for strength and resilience within the civil society structure in any given context.[xl]

While this book has focussed on elaborating the 'five functions framework', capacity building is the enabler of these functions. But how capacity building is done requires attention. Capacity building should strengthen a range of civic actors: organisations and groups of organisations or networks. Analytical, relational and transformational capacities should be built. Capacity building should empower sovereign CSO actors – the process of capacity building is as important as the outcome. Put another way, the process is the outcome.

---

[3] The dominance of global civil society by a few large associations does not necessarily favour, and may even preclude, the growth of the type of civil society we recommend in this book, which is characterised by diversity, over-lapping membership, and democratic governance.

Examples of capacity building interventions for civil society at different levels

Level	Interventions
Cross-sector CSOs, public sector, private sector, international aid sector etc	Facilitating forums, conferences, round tables etc Joint training Facilitating joint planning Building capacity for dialogue
Sector CSOs in general	Institutional development Enabling environment of civil society laws CSO forums Codes of practice Support for NGO support organisations Building media awareness of the sector
Sub-sector/networks Groups of types of CSOs focused around thematic interests, geography, identity etc	Strengthening internal network functioning Building capacity for communications Consultancy building/resource mobilisation Facilitating platforms e.g. Poverty or HIV/AIDS Federations of CBOs Building capacity for local government reform and participation
Organisational Individual organisations, largely of the intermediate NGO or CSO type	Organisational Capacity Building e.g. internal governance and leadership development; programme management; systems development; constituency building etc.
Grassroots community based organisation As a sub-group of the above organisational level	As above but also: Empowerment, rights awareness training Capacity for community services provision
Individual	Literacy training Civics education Rights awareness raising Voter registration

i. Nurture civil society in countries that 'graduate' from aid

There is also a role in middle-income countries to assist civil society to fulfil the functions we have outlined. The wealth of many middle-income countries is unequally distributed. Hence there is a hidden 'third world' within countries that have ostensibly 'graduated' from aid. The attitudes of states towards these sections of society within them vary widely, from genuinely inclusive policies to outright discrimination on class, caste, race, ethnicity or religious grounds. Elitism and power remain pervasive in all societies, and civil society has constant roles to play, endlessly enhancing the 'civic-ness' of their polities.

Northern countries should remember that a sign of a healthy society is its willingness to extend solidarity towards other societies that can benefit from their experience and support. As our functions show, civil society promotes development that is more holistic than service delivery for poverty reduction; international solidarity does not and should not stop when countries reach middle-income status. This does not necessarily entail large funding but it does mean strategic support, especially where certain areas, groups, or rights are prejudiced against. Continuing work to strengthen civil society in middle-income countries should be cherished as an international asset to empower the marginalised, deepen democracy, prevent conflict, and promote human rights. There should be funding available for civil society in middle-income countries with high inequality and poor governance – see for example our recommendations to 'be innovative about funding'.

7.4 Conclusions: towards sustainable civil society

Civil society is bigger than aid. To support civil society is more developmental than much of what passes as development, as the five functions are all intrinsically important to building cohesive societies and states, where inequality and poverty are constantly being tackled by a range of actors. Having explored these functions we argue that they have a strong universal importance regardless of whether people agree with the details of their origins and history. There are few, if any, societies that will not benefit from trying to enhance the capacity of civil society to fulfil these functions. Throughout this book we have shown that there are many opportunities for making these functions work better in the most varied contexts. We have also made several strategic and practical recommendations on how to strengthen civil societies. Here we conclude with a reminder of the key insights of the book.

> **Key implications for the five functions**
>
> 1. In order for associational life to create the **social basis of democracy**, civil society organisations need to build upon their own traditions of connecting with citizens and building networks with one another. External support can play an enabling role, but this must follow the impetus and power to drive social change which comes from within civil society.
>
> 2. Wide and deep relationships between different local actors are necessary to open up civic space and channels to demand **political accountability**, if we are to strengthen this local capacity nuanced and contextualised support may be required.
>
> 3. When building **social capital** in situations of injustice, the power of membership organisations is reliant on solidarity between the oppressed to act effectively for change in society. In fragile democracies, building horizontal networks in civil society, facilitated by new technology, can build relational capacities that last beyond specific campaigns, and may later transform into political capacities.
>
> 4. Developing **alternatives** highlights the important role of civil society in tackling status quo power relations, and the need for those working in and with civil society to have the courage and determination to risk testing different ideas without necessarily knowing the results in advance.
>
> 5. There are constant challenges around supporting marginalised groups. In promoting the **rights of citizens and the concept of citizenship**, civil society must be alert to governments that see no benefit in an autonomous civic arena. It is important to support citizen-based groups to claim civic space for collective action because purely 'unscripted civic action' favours the elite.

'Beyond NGOs' and back to membership bases

For more than a decade, seasoned observers and commentators have remarked that civil society essentially resides in membership associations of a wide variety of types, ranging from community based organisations at the grassroots, to mass membership associations such as trade unions, faith organisations and issue-based social movements. Although we have focused primarily on the functions of civil society, these organisational forms are important as they influence action. They also have the legitimacy, roots and capacity to transform societies, which is also why it so important that they should possess robust capacities. Although policy makers and some practitioners within the aid industry have understood this, the reality is that non-membership organisations dominate the funded part of the civic sector and have entrenched their position at the expense of membership organisations. NGOs and their networks have joined quasi-non-governmental bodies, think tanks and the like as the 'tail that wags the civic dog'. As a result NGOs are tempted to go way beyond the remit of offering support in solidarity with other civil societies.

For example, where membership-based organisations undertake service delivery, it usually has political potential, and where they undertake advocacy, it is very much rooted in the needs of their members. Where NGOs undertake either purely advocacy or service delivery 'on behalf' of their constituents, we have seen that it can be problematic, as either a technical exercise divorced from the wider political context, or as heavy handed and interventionist. Experience has shown that it is a small aspirational step for NGOs to shift from support to civil society to then setting the agenda and then 'operationalising' that agenda. Along the way membership starts falling off as potential activists decide to leave the job to the new 'professionals'. To avoid such apathy from spreading, the 'civic dog' needs to get its 'NGO tail' back under control.

Strengthen civil society as a whole

Mature civil societies have an institutional presence at different levels, arising from the multiplicity of relationships and interactions between the associations, organisations and individuals of which it is composed. We have also seen how nurturing civil society is an end in itself over and above any immediate benefits gained from supporting it. A strong civil society shapes and underpins the state, promoting civility and peace. Seeking to exploit civil society for subsidiary aims and objectives, however worthy in themselves, misunderstands its nature. A view of the intrinsic value of civil society as a whole should lead to an emphasis on strengthening networks between different parts of civil society. As the cases have shown, South–South cooperation and the use of new technology can be very effective in facilitating participatory, equal and mutual capacity building across civil society. Any interventions must remember that civil society is not just about providing services or just about advocating for political change – its primary role and function is to safeguard a democratic society of behalf of its citizens.

Civic space for the marginalised

The cases have powerfully illustrated that the 'enabling environment' for civil society means far more than just legal provision for CSOs to associate, gain operational resources, achieve voice and negotiate. These are useful approaches to enhancing the position of civil society in relation to the state, but we are more concerned about who gains access to this privileged space and how. Everywhere the marginalised are inadequately represented, usually because their access to these spaces is 'invited', if they have it all, and managed by intermediaries – such as NGOs. This reflects a general lack of power or agency to transform their lives. As we have seen though, there are promising signs that previously unheard groups are insisting on being heard and are creating civic space. Amongst these are squatters' associations, indigenous peoples' organisations and people with HIV/AIDS. These are often supported by media that is sensitive to issues of social exclusion and discrimination. It is through gaining such civic space that marginalised people can obtain equal rights and reduce structural poverty. Actively challenging the power dynamics that constantly allow elite monopolisation of civic space is difficult, and perhaps the simplest way is to support those groups who are 'making and shaping' civic space and respond to their definition of their needs and rights.

Rights as a catalyst

In the right context, the law has offered the marginalised a powerful tool to challenge endemic discrimination and social injustice. The 'right to have rights' has proved a rallying call for Brazil's urban homeless (see Chapter 4, page 55), providing their associations with the confidence to create spaces to be heard, assert agency and set about transforming their lives. This case was a good example of civil society fulfilling its functions, not as technical extension of professional NGOs' work, but rather using rights effectively for themselves. In a promising development of south-south cooperation, we have also seen the sharing of expertise amongst movements of victims that confront the problem of forced disappearances in Latin America, Asia and Africa (see Chapter 3, page 39).

Towards a civic role for INGOs

There are clear choices facing INGOs that aspire to strengthening civil societies. They involve painful decisions related to, amongst others, scale and type of operations, strategy and approach, marketing and fundraising. Our criticisms of INGOs in this book are not premised on the idea that INGOs are necessarily problematic. Rather, we criticise the current status quo, where market approaches dominate values-based action that is based in equal debate and ownership by northern and southern actors. INGOs need to adapt to the complex demands of helping to strengthen local civil societies and their representative organisations, along the lines of the recommendations we have made earlier in this chapter. Many INGOs have prioritised their own growth, but civil society strengthening requires a different approach – one which will involve sacrificing scale for solidarity. Appropriate aid to local civil society can pay dividends, as we saw from the impressive growth of civil society in Latin America, despite the inauspicious origins of aid under military dictatorships in the 1970s. Local CSOs should be allowed to take the lead in forging their own civil societies, in spite of the temptation for NGOs to 'do it themselves'. This will entail, amongst other things, a greater tolerance for flexibility and risk in dealings with partners who must be given as much autonomy as possible.

There are no easy ways for INGOs to reinvent themselves. Local civil societies need to be the main protagonists in all the five functions of civil society if they are to do a thorough job. INGOs should not use their international influence and resources to create spaces for themselves within local civil societies; they should ensure that they are invited by their southern partners. However there is a great deal they can do in building on the best practices learned through partnership approaches, extending the hand of solidarity to counterparts in the south, sharing resources or expertise in strengthening the environment for civil society and CSOs' 'existence, engagement and expression'.[xl]

Prioritise building 'sovereign capacities'

We have seen how the complexity of strengthening CSOs and structures, the expense involved and the long-term nature of the undertaking have contributed to a weakening of resolve and support for essential institutional (sector-wide) and organisational capacity building. The five functions described in this book are implemented by movements and associations that require appropriate organisational development to gain the influence and competence to make a sustainable contribution to the transformation of their societies. We have mentioned the crucial importance of relational capacities for swelling popular movements through building coalitions and networks amongst multitudes of CSOs. To achieve such movements individual CSOs need a range of capacities, for example to envision, govern, plan, learn, adapt and so on, whilst also mobilising membership and resources to push for change. We suggest that the fundamental vocation of non-membership NGOs is to accompany membership groups and CSOs as they progressively acquire these capacities and competencies.

Aim for a sustainable civil society

The ultimate aim is to move towards an autonomous civil society, actively engaged in all five civic functions, and in pursuit of broad visions of what society can and should be like. The need for this is vividly illustrated by those middle-income countries which are still facing the need for strong citizen organisations to challenge and reshape the state. We started this book by arguing that the major constraints for most poor people to move out of poverty have their origins in the political economies in which they live. Hence we have tried to show that we need a new way of thinking about poverty and about the roles of NGOs and other CSOs. The five functions of civil society provide a framework to analyse the roles and strengths of existing CSOs and ways of supporting them.

The challenge remains of how to provide capacity building to serve the goal of building autonomous civil societies without our interventions hindering that process. Running through many of our cases is the lesson that good practice is about strong partnerships which do not tread on local autonomy. There is scope for further exploration of past, present and future experiences of partnership – the promise and potential of which have not yet been fully delivered for the benefit of civil society and poor people worldwide.

To answer our first question 'whatever happened to civil society?', we have explored our framework through a series of case studies and sometimes contested theoretical models. We will in future be looking for more examples and hope to be able to provide a platform for sharing them. There are initiatives which have stood the test of time; whether through support to trade unions, indigenous groups, the cooperative movement, associations of disabled people: the list is endless and impressive. Civil society is complex, vulnerable to co-optation, prone to come in and out of fashion, certainly divided – but it is still vibrant, and it is not going to go away. The challenge remains to support civil society in countries with repressive governments, poor governance and high internal inequalities.

Appendix 1

Beyond NGOs: Components of civil society – distinguishing between NGOs, CSOs and social movements

This book repeatedly urges practitioners to engage with civil society 'beyond NGOs' – to reach out beyond the 'normal suspects' of NGOs, their networks and umbrella organisations, to the vast arena of membership organisations within civil society. The most basic generic typology of civil society contrasts membership organisations that 'help their members' with non-membership organisations that 'help others' – with a third category of uncivil organisations that 'help themselves'. The box below gives a list of 16 types of CSOs 'beyond NGOs', which were identified in a previous publication.[i]

Examples of civil society organisations active in development
- Membership-based religious organisations (congregations)
- Religious organisations that offer services to the general public
- Traditional indigenous community organisations
- Community organisations induced by outsiders
- Ethnic or tribal organisations
- Employment-based organisations:
    - Trade unions
    - Trade associations
    - Employer's organisations
    - Business associations
- Civic issues organisations
- Sports associations
- Culture associations
- Trusts and foundations
- Local area development organisations (or hometown associations)
- Advocacy and campaigning organisations (issue-based organisations)
- Social movements

Engaging 'beyond NGOs', is a call for development practitioners to thoroughly examine the fabric of local society. Just how dense this can be is born out by an INTRAC study in Ethiopia, which in a given locality mapped 31 types of civil society associations, only three of which were NGOs (see Appendix 3). Others included kin-based or neighbourhood-based mutual assistance associations, such as agricultural work groups; faith-based organisations; and broad-based CSOs such as clan and age group structures, service cooperatives and women's associations.

In her typology, Mary Kaldor calls civil society organisations 'social organisations' and draws a strong distinction between NGOs, which are about relief and development (through service provision and advocacy), and social movements, which address emancipation. Kaldor notes that her categories overlap, but states that they are useful in thinking about accountability. For Kaldor, social movements are the most progressive elements of civil society and potentially most accountable to the poor and excluded. She feels they emerged towards the end of the 1990s, led in the West by anti-globalisation (although there were many social movements which predate this period, as we note in the foreword).

Kaldor's typology of civil society actors[ii]				
	Social movements	NGOs	Social organisations	Nationalist and religious groups
Mission	Emancipation of the poor and excluded	Development and humanitarian relief	Protection and promotion of members' interests	Empowerment of national and religious groups
Activities	Protests, demonstrations and media events	Service provision and advocacy	Service provision, lobbying	Mobilisation through media, religious organisations and sometimes violence
Social composition	Activists, committed individuals, students	Professional staff	Workers, farmers, employers, local communities, displaced persons	Newly urbanised groups, peasants
Forms of organisation	Loose horizontal coalitions, networks	Ranges from bureaucratic and corporate, to small scale and informal	Ranges from vertical and hierarchical, to informal networks	Vertical and hierarchical although can nvolve networks of tightly organised cells, charismatic leadership

David C Korten also saw peoples' movements as the future of development strategy, replacing NGOs which had pursued the three previous generations of strategy: relief and welfare; then community development; then sustainable systems. Korten's framework seems to be being largely borne out by reality: there is a huge growth of social movements working for global change. But he had not foreseen the phenomenal and simultaneous growth in all of his four generations. For him development theorists and practitioners had to think beyond 'repair work', as social movements were not driven by budgets or organisational structures, but rather by ideas, by a vision of a better world. Also, while different CSOs might situate their strategies predominantly within one of Korten's generations, in practice they often combine different roles from each generation at any one time. They can, for example, combine community development with global advocacy. This reflects the fact that civil society is a highly contextualised phenomenon, and is always changing.

Korten's strategies of development-oriented NGOs: four generations[iii]				
	First **Relief and welfare**	Second **Community development**	Third **Sustainable systems development**	Fourth **People's movements**
Problem definition	Shortage	Local inertia	Institutional and policy constraints	Inadequate mobilising vision
Time frame **Scope**	Immediate Individual or family	Project life Neighbourhood or village	10–20 years Region or nation	Indefinite future National or global
Chief actors	NGO	NGO plus community	All relevant public and private institutions	Loosely defined networks of people and organisations
NGO role	Doer	Mobiliser	Catalyst	Activist/educator
Management orientation	Logistics management	Project management	Strategic management	Self-managing networks
Development education	Starving children	Community self-help	Constraining policies and institutions	Save the planet

Appendix 2

Who rules: The citizen or the state? Theoretical debates over civil society

The concept of civil society was not discovered by the aid industry sometime in the 1990s. It has a long and consistent history which goes back several hundred years. This Appendix give a brief overview of this thinking. We would argue that how you understand the relationship between the state and civil society will have implications for how this relationship works out in practice. Many development workers are undoubtedly unaware of the philosophy and its history which lies behind the way their daily work is framed, organised and structured. Many programmes may well not be explicitly tied to one or another approach to civil society as many governments may not be clear about the ideas which drive them to want to gain power: whether it is public service, personal gratification, personal wealth, family tradition, lack of alternative jobs, or endless other possibilities. What is reasonably clear is that the way the state regards itself: representing the people through a supreme leader or family; governing the ignorant from a point of view of better knowledge; performing a service on behalf of the population; representing different sectors of the population; all of these and more can be traced back to some very basic political ideas.

We are aware that this whole debate is heavily steeped in western thought about politics and philosophy, in which lie the origins of the concept of civil society. The dominance of an idea though does not mean that the practice is also a western construct – throughout this book there are many indigenous ideas and forms of organisation which we would define as belonging to civil society. Too often, autocratic and corrupt leaders have written off civil society as a western idea in an attempt to divert attention from their abuse of power.

This book jumps straight into issues around civil society's role and the practice of engaging with it – based on specific conceptual positions taken by the authors, which direct the reader to a certain approach. In this Appendix, we explore the range of views of civil society which have different cultural, intellectual and political origins, and bring with them different value sets and approaches to politics. Whilst summarising these different approaches, it is worth remembering that the very idea of a plural civil society that we take, following a Gramscian approach, should mean there is space for these alternative approaches to interact, compete and influence one another. Different agencies will inevitably take different approaches to civil society, which may derive from their origins or institutional relationships.

1. Who rules: the citizens or the state?

It is through the debate about the relationship between the state and the citizen that several clear ideas emerge which are still underpinning many of today's approaches towards civil society in different parts of the world. Some saw **the state as dominant** over the citizen, whether by a metaphorical contract whereby the citizen nominally or theoretically agrees to this, or, for example, by the divine right of the monarchy. Civil society, having 'agreed' to the sovereignty of the state, should obey the state. This system can be seen in the contemporary world, from the supreme leader in North Korea and other totalitarian states, through to some traditional leadership systems based on inheritance and monarchies. Even nominally democratic societies still sometimes need to be reminded that they exist to serve the citizen, not the reverse. If you assume that the citizen individually, or collectively as civil society, is subservient to the state then the accountability of the state to the citizen is not necessarily essential. If, however, you assume that the state is indeed in power at the behest of the citizen, then holding the state accountable is crucial. Therefore we have stressed that the **first function of civil society is to hold the state to account**. The state is a product of, and serves, its populace rather than the other way around. Even in neoliberal western democracies some politicians do not accept or understand this approach which is why they often depoliticise and weaken this relationship of the state and civil society – as per the JF Kennedy example 'not to ask what your country can do for you but you can do for your country'. There is a strong 'populist' tradition in more conservative or neoliberal western democracies which often fail – intentionally or not – to uphold the idea of the state serving the citizen in a two-way relationship of rights and obligations, instead stressing a one-way relationship of the citizen supporting the state.

Alternatively some have seen the social contract as **led by citizens**. This idea led utilitarian and libertarian thinkers to argue that the state is only the deliverer of limited purposes and that its legitimacy rests on it delivering those purposes. Democracy therefore provides a way for the citizen to change the government in charge of the state. Civil society provides the mechanism for multiple interests to emerge and lobby both the state and fellow citizens. Building on this we can see that another view is that of the **state is an arbiter** between these competing interests mediated through democratic processes.

2. The political origins of civil society – beyond an economic approach

During the 1990s there was an emphasis on the economic role of civil society and its 'not for profit' contribution to employment (whether voluntary and paid), services and products.[iv] Thus, politically, civil society was understood as the 'non-profit element of the market'. Indeed many domestic charities in developed and, increasingly, developing countries have colluded in the privatisation of services by competing to offer them on contract to the state. Throughout the book there is criticism of the problems that have been caused by such 'instrumentalised' civil society groups which are reduced to service delivery mechanisms controlled by the state, or international aid, and in doing so have reduced the wider and socio-political aspects and purposes of civil society.

Whilst the idea that democracy, the free market and civil society are interlinked dates back to Ricardo and Adam Smith's views it is indisputable that the original concept of civil society has political origins. Some would take this as far back as Greek city-states, where early civil society was characterised by the individual (male) citizens who gathered to make decisions in a democratic manner. However, many of the modern concepts of civil society date back to the debates on the nature of the state and its relationship to the citizen in France and Britain from the 17th and 18th centuries. The following sections focus on a number of the relevant writers, which illustrate the debates that are still current in our contemporary setting.

3. The citizens surrender their rights to a supreme leader

Hobbes (1588–1679) stated that 'life is nasty, brutish and short'. He claimed that conflict is inherent in self-protection, and that war and a lack of security will predominate unless a 'social contract' is set up to guarantee our security. This social contract entails humans placing restraints on themselves through mutual agreement or covenant. Therefore we compromise some freedoms – to exploit, conquer, rape and pillage – in return for our own security from others. Hobbes saw this contract between citizens, who choose by majority a sovereign to rule over them. Arguably, in the modern world we still see societies or groups which have not found agreement in such a 'social contract', hence the lawlessness and armed militias in places such as Somalia or the Pakistani tribal areas. Whilst on the other had we see autocrats, such as in Burma or North Korea, who believe they have the right to keep citizens under their control (benign or otherwise) for what they would argue is the common and greater good.

Crucially Hobbes, unlike **Locke** and **Rousseau** later, thought that although the citizen is then bound by the contract, there in no contract between the sovereign and citizens, and therefore the sovereign may decide what the rights of the citizen are. The problem is that this argument tends towards supporting an authoritarian system (at that time the monarchy) and reduces the need for countervailing power of say the courts or parliament. In this approach the worst despotism is regarded as still better than anarchy. Hobbes saw representation or accountability as meaningless unless backed by sovereign power, which could guarantee security. There is also an assumption of homogenous interests within the populace which underplays class and other differences.

Hobbes' approach is probably a good description of many states today which regard their power as absolute, with anything approaching democracy being given by the state to the citizen, rather than emerging from any inherent right of the citizen. Sadly, there are many examples of this form of absolutism, from Middle Eastern monarchies through to military dictatorship in Burma, the Chinese single party system, and African dictators in places like Equatorial Guinea and Zimbabwe.

Rousseau's (1712–1778) idea of the social contract looks, at first reading, close to

Locke but his justification for some forms of absolute power goes closer to Hobbes. Rousseau saw sovereignty as residing not in a ruler, but the body of citizens as a whole – the 'general will' is the sovereign. Whilst in some ways civil society and associations are the element of personal interest which is shared by others, and a vehicle for collective rights, what he didn't seem to allow for was differences of opinion in the general will. Thus it could be argued that Rousseau was against 'partial societies' within the state, and his view of the 'general will' as always being right and having legitimacy to rule can lead to despotism if one person or body successfully claims to represent such a general will. Whereas current ideas of civil society look to diversity and pluralism, you can see why some see his ideas providied one dubious justification for the totalitarianisms of the 20th century Europe, where Nazis and communists claimed a monopoly of interpretations of the general will.

We accept, however, that even where the state accepts the role of the citizen and civil society, this does not come automatically, and we have seen the effects of imperfect democracy in various regions across the world. Thus our second function is about the role of civil society in providing the basis for social and political democracy by providing experience of basic democratic practices to enable people to fulfil these functions at a higher level and to create the culture of participation rather than oppression.

4. Associations of citizens are important to uphold a just social contract

Locke (1632–1704) moved away from idea of the sovereign having an absolute, or divine, power, whilst still accepting the ideas of Hobbes about a social contract being necessary for security and society. For Locke, the key to his thinking about why citizens devised a contract with the government was the role of private property. Unlike Hobbes, Locke argued that political power existed for the public good – defence of property, life and from foreign interference – and if rulers failed in their part of the contract then it was legitimate to resist or seek a change in government.

He also argued that there should be a division between the executive, legislature and judiciary, constituting the division of powers which still dominate many forms of democracy. It is through Locke that we see the emergence of associations within civil society as important, because it is through associations that citizens can demand justice from the state, or elect a different power. Underlying some of Locke's ideas was the older concept of the moral restraints on power as responsible for the community it governs. As we mention in the main text there is historically a close parallel between ideas of social capital and trust, and the defence of property. What some would argue as one of the first acts of civil society to control unbridled power in 1214 where the Lords made the King of England sign the Magna Carta, was in reality as much about protecting private property from the King. Thus our third function is keenly related to building trust between groups and individuals, about the diversity and plurality of civil society and the positives this has for social, and indeed commercial, life.

5. The state exists because citizens collectively accept it

Unhappy with the idea of the social contract being made and accepted by individuals, **Hume (1711–1776)** and others concluded that the acceptance of the state derived from its utility to its citizens. Therefore because the state provides a service to citizens we obey it; the legitimacy of the state is generated by citizens' collective acceptance of it. We explore this in our chapter on citizenship (our fifth function). Given that the alternative is anarchy, the utilitarian response was to make the state work more efficiently. At the time that Hume was writing, many states saw the growth of parliament, democratic voting, free press and many of the trappings of democracy designed to ensure that the state provided useful services to civil society.

In some ways the current set of ideas that the state should provide a set of services to the individual, whether these are couched in terms of social services, rights, or security, derives from the concept that the citizen obeys the state because it provides what they need. If the state is seen to be unable or unwilling to deliver such services then, at one end of a spectrum, is the rejection of the government of the day via democratic means and, at the other end, the violent rejection of the government and possibly the state as well, leading to civil war and forced migration. It is clear that the northern European concepts of the welfare state, and the resulting approaches to international development owe a lot to the utilitarian idea that the state should deliver and citizens should ensure that it does so.

6. Civil society provides all, supervised by the higher moral order of the state

It was **Hegel (1770–1831)** who developed a clear idea of civil society as both a contrast to the state and mutually interdependent with it. The state, as Hegel conceived it, is not a utilitarian institution engaged in the common place business of providing public services, administering the law, performing police duties and adjusting economic interests. He argued that all these areas belong to civil society. The state may direct and regulate them as the need arises, but it does not itself perform them. Civil society depends on the state for intelligent supervision and moral significance. The state however depends upon civil society for the means of accomplishing moral purposes which it embodies.[v] But he saw civil society as a lesser order, assuming the state would act above the baser individualist instincts of civil society. The law, as an embodiment of rationalist thought, helped ensure this balance and control on the state. The law as a way of ensuring control over the state was taken up by non-religious radicals like **Bentham** and **Mill** who argued for legal reform in favour of maintaining individual liberty. Thus the focus on the individual citizen came to the fore. This is still with us today in the form of both the rights-based approaches to development and the North American concept that the state should be minimal and that civil society should deliver services wherever possible with minimal state regulation and intervention. This is often followed up by a focus on the law as a means of governing relationships with the state.

7. Civil society and the state – a transatlantic divide

There are at least two divides either side of the Atlantic in how civil society is viewed. The first is that the ideas of **Tocqueville (1805–1859)**, written before the American Civil War, embedded the idea in America that grassroots democracy allowed local and other interests to resolve issues locally and democratically without the violence of European wars and revolutions. Therefore civil society is seen as more useful than the state in devising policies, and providing services and resolving problems. Linked to this, the second divide is that the state is thus regarded differently. In North America, the seemingly logical argument is that a small conservative state should leave communities to get on with their own business. The European 'radical' model, on the other hand, called for intervention to ensue greater equality of class, race and gender. To this extent the state was called to ensure this recognition of these 'minority' rights or the rights of the majority when oppressed by minority elites. It is possible to characterise the North American approach as one which values the small state, and regards civil society as existing to keep the state from growing and extending itself. IN contrast, in northern Europe civil society is considered essential to ensure that the state delivers its promises whether in terms of social, education, health or welfare, or guarantees of minority rights. Here, the state delivers and civil society lobbies for these services and monitors their application. Different stances on healthcare epitomise this divide; for Europeans the idea that people would argue against universal health care seems to go against all common sense, whereas for many Americans the European model has been branded as 'communist inefficiency gone mad'.

Appendix 3

Example of civil society mapping in Ethiopia

Category		Membership or not membership-based, role and function
	Sub-category	
1. Kin-based or neighbourhood-based mutual assistance		Membership-based
1.1	Agricultural work groups – *dafo, debo, wonfel*	Provision of an organised workforce for labour intensive, seasonal and often monotonous tasks
1.2	Livestock (cattle) herding groups	Collective rearing and herding of livestock
1.3	Tree planting groups	Coordinated provision of labour for the production, sale and planting of seedlings
1.4	Water users' group	Mobilisation and organisation of labour for water source maintenance and development (often organised by the *kebele* cabinet)
1.5	Butter groups, e.g. *qib-yidemuji*	Provision of labour on a rotating basis for the production of butter
1.6	Burial associations, *iddir* and multi-purpose *iddir*	Members contribute to ensure a proper burial for themselves and their relatives. Burial costs are met from a common fund and members also contribute food, drink at funerals, and provide social and religious support to the bereaved family. Multi-purpose *iddir* provide funds for emergencies, in addition to burials
1.7	Rotating savings and credit, e.g. *iqqub*	Provision of access to large sums of money (for house construction, starting a small business etc)
1.8	Producers' cooperatives	Collective organisation of cultivation, fishing or gathering or forest products
1.9	Grain groups	Provision of grain to members on low interest loans in months of scarcity
1.10	Seed banks	Provision of seed on low interest loans
1.11	Neighbourhood watch, e.g. *qerator/mozoya*	For the protection of property – organised on a rotation basis
2. Neighbourhood faith-based		Membership-based
2.1	Burial associations, *iddir*	As above

2.2	Rotating feast groups which celebrate a saint's day – *mahaber* (EOC)	Through celebrating the life of a saint, to strengthen religious life/ relations and to provide economic and social support in times of need (in some *mahaber*) and for wedding (in some *mahaber*). A saint's day falls at once a month, sometimes twice. Mahaber may also function as a means of reconciliation between quarrelling members.
2.3	Rotating sabbath day group, which celebrates with beer and bread after church – *sembete* (EOC)	As above, but through regular celebration after church services.
2.4	Mosque congregation – *jemma*	Lead by the *khadi* (religious leader), the *jemma* can raise funds and provide assistance to households in need, and to other *jemma* for projects.
2.5	Funeral contributions from households, which are made to the mosque – *ezen*	This is more of an event than an organisation: it functions as an institution in the provision of food for the seven days of a funeral.
3. Broad-based, which functions in an area larger than a neighbourhood		Membership based, although in some organisations/institutions this may be through membership of the clan or sub clan (e.g. in natural resource management). Not all women and youth in the *kebeles* are members of the women and youth organisations, but these associations are membership-based.
3.1	Umbrella multi-purpose *iddir*– also know as *modi*	Coordination of activities of member *iddirs*, in particular to allow the flow of resources between *iddir*. Some also have a conflict mediation role.
3.2	Natural resource management organisations, e.g. grazing groups, clan and sub-clan based water and pasture management in pastoral and agro-pastoral societies	Management of natural resources. Representative function in some areas, where the clan and sub clan structure actively represents the interests of members, e.g. the *Ghada* in Borana society (Liben) and amongst the Somali (Shinile) and Afar (Dubti).
3.3	Service cooperatives	Provision of local services – supply of inputs, agro processing and the marketing of produce.
3.4	*Kebele* association	The lowest formal, discrete unit of mass organisation: all registered *kebele* residents are members. Representative function, although this is often limited to working within given government policy.
3.5	Women's associations	For the collective organisation of women for development projects. For the representation of women's interests at kebele and woreda level, but not all *kebeles* have women's associations.

APPENDIX 3

3.6	Youth associations	Very similar role and function to the women's associations. Not all *kebeles* have youth associations. Many have a strong interest in sports and sexual health (HIV/AIDS).
3.7	Clan, sub-clan and age group structures	Clan and sub-clan Natural resource management – see above. Conflict resolution/peace building mechanisms are particularly strong amongst pastoral and agro-pastoral peoples Age groups In Baco Gazer the 'junior' age group has mutual assistance agricultural groups, and the elders perform rituals for the well being of the community. Another means of settling disputes.
3.8	Business/trade group	*Injera* Makers Solid Waste Collectors' Association Shoe Shiner's Club Weaver's Association Workers' Association Women's home economi. Dubti Tendaho Cotton Loaders Association Weaytu Public and Freight Transport Association Carters' Association – provide cart service to the public
3.9	Professional	Baco Gazer, Gimbo Teachers' Association
4. Service providers		Micro finance and service cooperatives are membership based, but most service providers are not.
4.1	Micro finance/credit	Provision of larger sums of credit, than that available through *iqqub*.
4.2	Service cooperatives	Provision of local services – the supply of inputs, agro processing and the marketing of produce.
4.3	Private sector, in particular health service providers	Used in the absence of government services.
5. NGO		Ethiopian and international NGOs
5.1	Development associations	All exist to represent the interests of members, and the largest role is in service delivery.
5.2	Ethiopia NGOs	At *kebele* and *woreda* levels roles and function lie predominantly in service delivery.
5.3	International NGOs	At *kebele* and *woreda* levels roles and function lie predominantly in service delivery.

Adapted from Muir, A.(2004) *INTRAC Study for The World Bank Building: Capacity in Ethiopia to Strengthen the Participation of Citizens' Associations in Development: A Study of the Organizational Associations of Citizens*, Oxford: INTRAC
www.intrac.org/data/files/resources/657/Building-Capacity-in-Ethiopia-to-Strengthen-the-Participation-of-Citizens-Associations-in-Development.pdf

Chapter endnotes

Chapter 1

i Pratt, B. (2009) 'INTRAC Briefing Paper 24: Civil Society and Development – Challenges from European Governments?', Oxford: INTRAC. www.intrac.org/resources.php?action=resource&id=658

Giffen, J. and Judge, R. (2010) 'Civil Society Policy and Practice in Donor Agencies', INTRAC: Oxford. www.intrac.org/resources.php?action=resource&id=681

ii Brehm, V.M. with E. Harris-Curtis, L. Padrao, and M. Tanner (2004) *Autonomy or Dependence? Case Studies of North-South NGO Partnerships*, Oxford: INTRAC. www.intrac.org/resources.php?action=resource&id=319

Fowler, A. (2000) Partnerships – Negotiating Relationships: A resource for NGOs (OPS 32), Oxford: INTRAC. www.intrac.org/resources.php?action=resource&id=54

iii Commission of Inquiry into the Future of Civil Society in the UK and Ireland (2010) *Making Good Society*, Carnegie UK Trust. http://democracy.carnegieuktrust.org.uk/civil_society/publications/making_good_society

iv Benequista, N. *Putting States at the Centre: Linking States and Societies for Responsive Governance: A policy-maker's guide to the research of the Development Research Centre on Citizenship, Participation and Accountability*, Sussex: IDS and London: DFID. www.drc-citizenship.org/publications/CDRC_Policy_Findings_Summary.pdf

v Howell, J. and J. Pearce (2001) *Civil Society and Development: a Critical Exploration*. Boulder CO: Lynne Rienner Publishers Inc.

vi Commission of Inquiry into the Future of Civil Society in the UK and Ireland (2010) *Making Good Society*, Carnegie UK Trust.

Chapter 2

vii Van Rooy, A. (ed) (1998) *Civil Society and the Aid Industry*, London: Earthscan Ltd.

viii Cohen, J. and Arato, A. (1992) *Civil Society and Political Theory*, Cambridge: Massachusetts Institute of Technology.

ix Cabellero, A. (2008) 'Citizens' Initiative Programme in Paraguay', Unpublished Case Study from 2008 INTRAC Conference: 'Whatever Happened to Civil Society?', 3–5 December 2008, KDK Conference Centre, the Netherlands.

x Jones, B. (2008) 'Leading civil society up the governance path: civil society in Ethiopia as an instrument of "democratic structural adjustment"', Unpublished Case Study from 2008 INTRAC Conference: 'Whatever Happened to Civil Society?' 3–5 December 2008, KDK Conference Centre, the Netherlands.

Chapter 3

xi Tocqueville, A. (2000 [1835/40]), *Democracy in America*, H. C. Mansfield and D. Winthrop (trans and eds). Chicago: University of Chicago.

xii Tulod-Peteros, C. (2008) 'Human Rights of the Disappeared and their families: The Experiences of Asian Federation Against Involuntary Disappearances (AFAD)', Unpublished Case Study from 2008 INTRAC Conference: 'Whatever Happened to Civil Society?', 3–5 December 2008, KDK Conference Centre, the Netherlands.

xiii Gervais, C. (2008) 'How Child Rights National Coalitions in Latin America have used the mechanisms of the Inter-American Commission on Human Rights to provide State accountability', Unpublished Case Study from 2008 INTRAC Conference: 'Whatever Happened to Civil Society?', 3–5 December 2008, KDK Conference Centre, the Netherlands.

Chapter 4

xiv Diamond, L. (1999) *Developing Democracy: Towards Consolidation*, Baltimore: Johns Hopkins Press.

xv Fukuyama, F. (2001) 'Social Capital, Civil Society and Development', *Third World Quarterly* 22(1):7–20.

Foley, M. and B. Edwards (1999) 'Is it Time to Disinvest in Social Capital?', *Journal of Public Policy* 19(2):141–71.

xvi Earle, L. (2004) *Social Movements and NGOs: A Preliminary Investigation*, Oxford: INTRAC. www.intrac.org/resources.php?action=resource&id=31

xvii Film makers Glen Elis and Kay Bishop, quoted in Ken Saro-Wiwa Foundation (2005) *If I live to tell the tale*, Ken Saro-Wiwa Foundation Publication.

xviii INTRAC Effective Relations Workshop, Bishkek, March 14–16, 2006. Case study by Mamurkhon Akramov, Agency_Nau, with John Beauclerk.

xix Beauclerk, J. and R. Holloway (2007) 'Beyond NGOs, Civil society organisations with development impact: Case studies compiled by the AKDN Civil Society Programme and INTRAC', AKDN. *www.akdn.org/publications/civil_society_beyond_ngos.pdf*

Chapter 5

xx Bebbington, A.J., S. Hickey and D.C. Mitlin, eds. (2008) *Can NGOs Make a Difference? The Challenge of Development Alternatives*, London: Zed Books.

xxi Sneller, A. (2008) 'Who we think we are: women as managers and leaders in International Development', Unpublished Case Study from 2008 INTRAC Conference: 'Whatever Happened to Civil Society?', 3–5 December 2008, KDK Conference Centre, the Netherlands.

xxii Howell, J. and J. Pearce (2001) *Civil Society and Development: a Critical Exploration*. Boulder CO: Lynne Rienner Publishers Inc.

Edwards, M. and A. Fowler (eds) (2002) *The Earthscan Reader on NGO Management*, London, Earthscan Publications Ltd.

Kaldor, M (2002) 'Civil Society and Accountability', *UNDP background paper for Human Development Report 2002*, UNDP. Accessed 30.12.09 at:
http://hdr.undp.org/en/reports/global/hdr2002/papers/Kaldor_2002.pdf

Chapter 6

xxiii Foweraker, J. and T. Landman (2000) *Citizenship Rights and Social Movements: A Comparative and Statistical Analysis*. Oxford: Oxford University Press. pp 29.

xxiv Civicus Civil Society Watch (2010) *E Civicus* 470, 15.1.2010.

xxv Armas, H. (2008) 'Citizens with HIV/AIDS. The challenges for participation and civil society in the Global Fund in Peru', Unpublished Case Study from 2008 INTRAC Conference: 'Whatever Happened to Civil Society?', 3–5 December 2008, KDK Conference Centre, the Netherlands.

xxvi Armas, H. (2008) 'Citizens with HIV/AIDS. The challenges for participation and civil society in the Global Fund in Peru', Unpublished Case Study from 2008 INTRAC Conference: 'Whatever Happened to Civil Society?', 3–5 December 2008, KDK Conference Centre, the Netherlands.

xxvii Cornwall, A. and J. Gaventa (2000) 'From users and choosers to makers and shapers: Repositioning participation in social policy.' *IDS Bulletin* 31 (4)

xxviii Compiled from reports posted on Servindi from early 2009, Servicios en Comunicación Intercultural Servindi. www.servindi.org

xxix Cornwall, A. and J. Gaventa (2000) 'From users and choosers to makers and shapers: Repositioning participation in social policy.' *IDS Bulletin* 31 (4)

xxx As argued by Boyte, H. (2008) 'Civic Driven Change and Developmental Democracy', in Fowler, A. and Biekart, K. (eds), *Civic Driven Change: Citizen's Imagination in Action*, The Hague: Institute of Social Studies.

Chapter 7

xxxi Salamon, L. M. and H. K. Anheier (1996) *The Emerging Nonprofit Sector: an Overview (Johns Hopkins Non-Profit Sector Series 1)*, Manchester: Manchester University Press.

xxxii Malena, C. (ed) (2009) *From Political Won't to Political Will: Building Support for Participatory Governance*, Johannesburg: CIVICUS.

Cornwall, A. and J. Gaventa (2000) 'From users and choosers to makers and shapers: Repositioning participation in social policy.' IDS Bulletin 31 (4)

xxxiii Crook, R. (2009) 'South-North non-governmental networks, policy processes and policy outcomes', Unpublished paper presented at INTRAC May 2009 NGO Research Forum

xxxiv Cornwall A. and J. Gaventa (2000) 'From users and choosers to makers and shapers: Repositioning participation in social policy'. IDS Bulletin 31 (4)

xxxv Howell, J. and J. Pearce (2001) Civil Society and Development: a Critical Exploration. Boulder CO: Lynne Rienner Publishers Inc.

Derksen, H. (2009) Challenges for Civil Society: Conference Report – Whatever Happened to Civil Society? Oxford: INTRAC.

xxxvi Treasure, K. (2009) 'When it's time to move beyond aid', Guardian Weekly 11.12.09

xxxvii Buxton, C. (forthcoming, 2011) *The Struggle for Civil Society in Central Asia: Crisis and Transformation*, Sterling, VA: Kumarian Press

Luttwak, E. (1999) *Turbo-Capitalism: Winners and Losers in the Global Economy*, New York: HarperCollins.

xxxviii Skocpol, T. (2003) *Diminishing Democracy: From Membership to Management in American Civic Life*, Norman, OK: Oklahoma University Press.

xxxix Danida, Ministry of Foreign Affairs Denmark (2008) *Strategy for Danish Support to Civil Society in Developing Countries: December 2008*, Danida, Ministry of Foreign Affairs Denmark, Copenhagen. www.ambdaressalaam.um.dk/NR/rdonlyres/EDE2C581-F01E-41EA-A977-CA6A0B4E13F0/0/571981_Civilsamfundsstrategien_UK_WEB.pdf

xl Lipson, B. and M. Hunt, (2008) *Capacity Building Framework: A values based programming guide*, Oxford: INTRAC

xli Fowler, A. (2003) 'An enabling environment for civil society: What does it mean and how does law fit in?' Centre for Civil Society Research Report 7: 1-14. www.nu.ac.za/ccs/default.asp?10,24,10,813

See also the World Bank's The ARVIN Framework: A Way to Assess the Enabling Environment for Civic Engagement: Association, Resources, Voice, Information and Negotiation, Washington DC: The World Bank.
http://web.worldbank.org/WBSITE/EXTERNAL/TOPICS/EXTSOCIALDEVELOPMENT/EXTPCENG/0,,contentMDK:20529003~pagePK:148956~piPK:216618~theSitePK:410306,00.html

International Center for Not-for-Profit Law (2003) ARVIN Descriptors, Washington DC: The World Bank.
http://siteresources.worldbank.org/INTPCENG/1220276-1118059556158/20526727/Descriptors+-
-+final.pdf

Appendices

i Beauclerk, J. and R. Holloway (2007) 'Beyond NGOs, Civil society organisations with development impact: Case studies compiled by the AKDN Civil Society Programme and INTRAC', AKDN. www.akdn.org/publications/civil_society_beyond_ngos.pdf

ii Kaldor, M. (2003), 'Civil Society and Accountability', Journal of Human Development, Vol 4, No 1, p12.

iii Korten, D. C. (1990) *Getting to the 21st Century: Voluntary Action and the Global Agenda*, Sterling, VA: Kumarian Press.

iv Howell, J. and J. Pearce (2001) Civil Society and Development: a Critical Exploration. Boulder CO: Lynne Rienner Publishers Inc.

Salamon, L. M. and H. K. Anheier (1996) *The Emerging Nonprofit Sector: an Overview* (Johns Hopkins Non-Profit Sector Series 1), Manchester: Manchester University Press.

v Sabine, G.H. and T. L. Thorson, (1980) *A History of Political Theory*, Fourth Edition, London: Thomson Learning.